CURTIS
SMITH

D0108434

Counseling Parents of
Hearing-Impaired Children

Curtis
Smith

Counseling Parents of Hearing-Impaired Children

David Luterman, D. Ed.

Professor of Communication Disorders,
Director, Thayer Lindsley Parent-Centered
Nursery for Hearing-Impaired Children,
Emerson College, Boston

Foreword BY MARK ROSS, Ph.D.

Professor of Audiology, Department of Speech
University of Connecticut, Storrs

Little, Brown and Company

Boston

Copyright © 1979 by Little, Brown and Company (Inc.)

First Edition

All rights reserved. No part of this book may be
reproduced in any form or by any electronic or
mechanical means, including information storage
and retrieval systems, without permission in
writing from the publisher, except by a reviewer
who may quote brief passages in a review.

Library of Congress Catalog Card No. 79-84419
ISBN 0-316-53750-0

Printed in the United States of America

To the parents
who have sustained me with their courage
and who have taught me so much

Contents

Foreword

At the time I entered the profession of audiology, most of its practitioners were drawn from the ranks of speech pathologists. At that time the prevailing assumption was that the field attracted those speech pathologists who felt more comfortable with instrumentation than with people or, perhaps, those who preferred short-term diagnostic encounters, which conferred a white-coat, "doctorlike" status on them rather than the emotional commitment implicit in a long-term therapeutic relationship. Many of us resented that assumption because it underestimated our own efforts and perceptions, and we have worked to stress the equally, if not more, important role of audiologists in educational and rehabilitation endeavors. This book by Dr. David Luterman is the most powerful expression of a humanistically oriented audiologist I have ever read. He is reminding us that between every set of headphones lies more than a pair of ears, and that in the last analysis it is human beings dealing with other human beings that affects, for better or worse, the human condition. It is a harbinger of the changing nature of the profession of audiology that such a book could be written by an audiologist; the receptivity and eagerness with which its message is accepted will test the current maturity of the profession.

The book, however, is aimed not just at audiologists, but at educators of the deaf and all other groups and individuals who bear diagnostic and therapeutic responsibilities for the young, hearing-impaired child. Dr. Luterman's primary message is clear: We must move beyond the temptation to view the parents of these children, at best, only as receptacles of our "wisdom" and, at worst, as obstacles and adversaries who must be overcome in order for us to "get through" to their children.

The parents are, for better or worse, the most important figures in their children's lives—their first, and unavoidably most important, "teachers." In the interests of the children, they cannot be shunted off to a secondary role. But beyond this perception, David Luterman views the parents as people who, overwhelmed and overwrought by the shattering impact of having a deaf child, require our assistance in terms of their own needs. Our clients are not just the children but their parents as well. Certainly, satisfying the needs and reducing the conflicts of the parents should help the children, but our concern for the parents is independent of (though derived from) them. Nevertheless, it is important to emphasize the almost symbiotic relationship that exists between a child and his parents (most clearly with the mother). As the parents work through their own feelings regarding their child, the impact on the child cannot help but be favorable and possibly result in improvements in the child's performance in some dimension; the corollary of this reasoning, of course, is that improvement in the child's performance, through perhaps the appropriate selection and utilization of amplification, may lessen parental anxiety. The reciprocity of the relationship between a child and his parents is an ever-present consideration in working with both the children and their parents, separately or simultaneously.

No one "system" is prescribed for parent involvement, nor is any one parent-infant program, nursery program, or communication mode advocated for all hearing-impaired children. Such an imposition on people would violate one of the basic themes permeating the book, and that is the explicit recognition of individual differences and circumstances. Dr. Luterman presents a number of models for organizing different types of programs, which involve different styles and degrees of parental involvement. Although he prefers the auditory-oral mode of communication, nowhere does that preference get elevated to a religious disputation; rather, his focus remains on the child and his parents, encompassing more fundamental concerns than the mode of communication, such as the child's psychosocial status, the relationship between the child and his parents, and, finally, the parents' acceptance of the reality of their own child's condition.

The book conveys another important message to those readers, mainly audiologists, educators of the deaf, or speech and language pathologists, whose professional mission requires that they provide direct and on-going therapy services to hearing-impaired children and their parents. It is a message that, in my experience, does not get much recognition or acceptance by members of those groups, the associations they belong to, or the institutions that train them. Its essence is contained in the quotation "Physician, heal thyself." Dealing as we do with some of the strongest human emotions and feelings, it is probable that the state of our own emotional well-being will somehow warp the therapeutic relationship. We are not mechanics dealing with machines. Our own personalities, our own needs, and our own deficiencies and strengths enter into our interactions with people and thereby modify our relationships with them. The healthier we are, the more we can enter the therapy process as "whole" persons, the more likely that our ostensible therapy goals are the actual ones, and not just a smokescreen within which our own hidden needs get satisfied. Too often we seem to find some colleagues operating as emotional scavengers, feeding on the dependencies of their clients to fill the emotional gaps in themselves. Professional growth should imply more than the mere accumulation of data, important as that process is; it should also imply the concurrent expansion of one's emotional vision into oneself.

No one I know in this field, or anywhere for that matter, is a better example of the sentiments I am expressing than David Luterman. Although writing about an author's personal qualities as a foreword to his book may not seem to be appropriate, those personal qualities represent a good deal of what this book is all about. Listen to him speak to you, the reader, through the words of this book; listen to his doubts, his self-examinations, his strivings always to understand himself, and, through himself, his clients; listen to him carefully and you will hear a therapist, in the true sense of the word— a healer—speaking to you. He would disclaim this title, saying that his efforts are devoted to helping people heal themselves by helping them remove the barriers from self-actualization.

We can perhaps visualize him best, and his lessons for us to emulate, as a gentle conductor, nudging his clients on the path to personal insight and growth but, at the same time, accompanying them on their path.

On a number of occasions in the past, I have had an opportunity to meet and talk to Dr. Luterman's "graduates," the parents who have completed his year-long program. They are a unique breed. Nowhere have I ever met parents of hearing-impaired children who demonstrated a more effective and realistic concern for the welfare of their children. There was also no lack of the information that traditional "counseling" programs emphasize in their work with parents; they were fully informed regarding language and speech development, hearing aids, and the pros and cons of different communication modes and educational placements. What distinguished them was their capacity to use that information realistically and to see its applicability to their children.

The active participation of such parents on the educational scene is an absolute necessity, more now than ever before. We are being inundated on the national, state, and local scenes with laws, regulations, and guidelines, all of which have apparently laudable purposes, but which also sometimes appear to impede rather than foster educational services and alternatives for hearing-impaired children. It is easy for the average parents, and educators as well, to simply become overwhelmed by the complexity of the regulations they are expected to observe. Programs and, by extension, children are judged by their conformance to those regulations (since this is a relatively easy task for members of the bureaucracy, thereby justifying their existence) and not by educational quality or educational progress. The children are being lost in a morass of red tape; they can best, in my judgment, be extracted from this predicament by the involvement of informed parents in the political process. The realization of that opportunity is a bonus consideration in programs such as Dr. Luterman's. In the long run, it may be the one that has the greatest impact for all hearing-impaired children.

This book, however, is basically not about bureaucrats, parents, children, or even professionals for that matter; it is about people who happen to wear different labels denoting a different status. For most of this book, David Luterman speaks universally to all of us, as a whole man giving us the lessons of his experiences, so that we may see ourselves more clearly and thus also see those entrusted to our care with more understanding.

MARK ROSS

Preface

During the past thirteen years, I have been directing a parent-centered nursery program conducted within a college setting. I began as a young audiologist with almost no information about deaf education and only vague insights into counseling issues. I have learned a great deal over these thirteen years—more from my failures, which were many, than from my successes, which seemed all too few or were seldom recognized by me. For me, as a professional, this book represents the outcome of my need to summarize, to reflect on what I have learned, and to try to share my experience with others. It is not intended as a scholarly document on parent education (there is not enough research material presently available to write such a book), but rather as a personal document which relates my experience as a clinician working with parents. Although my experience has been predominantly with parents of deaf children, I have little doubt that this material is applicable to any parent of a handicapped child and to the professional who is concerned with counseling and programming for the parent.

Since I have been exploring issues of parent counseling in various parts of the country, it has become apparent to me that there is a great deal of dissatisfaction on the parts of both the parents and the professionals concerning the role of parents in the educational process. On the one hand, I hear the professionals affirm, in the most sacred tones, the need to involve parents more; on the other hand, that theory is not effectively carried out in practice. The parents are often accorded second-class citizen status; that is, the parent-centered part of the program is appended to the child-centered aspect of the program and the parents receive merely the crumbs from the meal served to the child. The parents' involvement is often limited to the hurried conference after a therapy session, a yearly teacher conference, and, most often, an evening meeting once every few months that features a guest speaker. Invariably, attendance at such meetings is low and the embarrassed school administrator wrings his hands and bewails the "parental attitude."

The current policy for parent education in almost all cases appears to be school-based; that is, the school administration makes all decisions about what parents need to know and about how the information is to be presented. Parents are rarely acknowledged or consulted in designing their own educational experience. Very few educational programs are designed that focus on the parents. Usually, those programs that start out with a parent emphasis quickly become child-centered. It is not surprising that the parents do not attend meetings and that, consequently, the schools bemoan their "lack of interest."

In large part, the difficulty faced by parents and professionals involved in parent education results from a lack of adequate training in professional education programs. There is rarely any direct instruction on parent-related issues and there is almost never any training in how to deal with attitudes and feelings. As a result, the professional tends to "distance" the parents by keeping the relationship in content areas, in which he has the control. Although the professional verbalizes the need for parent involvement, his behavior contradicts his words, which results in continued ambiguity.

The parents approach the professional with equal ambivalence. Although they might verbalize a desire to participate and to have control over their child's schooling, in reality they usually want the professional to relieve them of their burden and to take over the responsibility for educating the child. The parents also approach the professional with accumulated angers and defenses from their own earlier educational experiences of dealing with teachers; such experiences, unfortunately, generally have tended to be negative, with the parent, as a result, feeling intimidated by the teacher and the school. Consequently, although parents *say* they want to participate in their child's educational program, and professionals *say* they want parents in their programs, there are still strong emotional barriers to effective communication that prevent or limit the establishment of effective programs of parent education.

This book is dedicated to the notion that parent education can be a viable vehicle for reaching the handicapped child if programs are established for the parents. A parent-centered program, however, must be seen as only one means for helping the hearing-impaired child achieve his potential; there are equally effective child-centered programs that will assume responsibility for managing the child. What the professional needs to ensure is that the community provides a variety of programs—some child-centered and some parent-centered—

and that the parents are allowed to choose the most suitable program for their individual families. The professionals already involved in a specific program must examine their attitudes to determine if they really want intense parent participation. If the answer is in the affirmative, then it is important that they work toward designing programs for the parents. I want to share my experiences of parent work with those professionals who are willing to make a commitment to parent education—who are interested in exploring issues of counseling and relating to parents in (perhaps) unconventional ways. I also hope to provide some help in the training of future professionals and in improving their dealings with parents.

A book such as this becomes obsolete the moment it is written. It is merely a signpost saying, "He went that way." With that caveat in mind, I wish you, the reader, "Good luck." For me, my work with parents has been an incredible, personally gratifying, and professionally rewarding experience.

D.L.

Acknowledgments

This book could not have been written without the help of many people. I am very grateful for the many helpful suggestions made by Judy Chasin and Susan Colten. I am also deeply indebted to Linda Dolmatch, who not only typed the manuscript, but was also in many ways a collaborator.

I express my deepest appreciation to Charles Klim, who gave me the personal and professional room in which to grow.

To my wife, Cari, who did so many things to make this book possible, including very careful editing of the manuscript, I give my deepest thanks.

To Alison, Daniel, Emily, and James, who had to put up with a more than usually distracted father, I thank you for your understanding.

And to my mother, just because . . .

A Matter of Pronouns

The problem of pronouns at this stage of our social consciousness is a formidable one. The constructs of his/her, and so forth, are so awkward that I have decided to make some arbitrary designations. Parents and teachers of the deaf are referred to as "she" in this book, only because it seems at this time to reflect the reality. I will refer to the counselor/audiologist as "he," since, in my own experience, that mirrors the present state of affairs. I also refer to the child as "he." For bureaucrats and school administrators who are not mentioned too frequently in the text, I have decided to be inconsistent. Admittedly, these designations are arbitrary and I look forward to the development of neuter singular pronouns.

Counseling Parents of Hearing-Impaired Children

1
The Parent in the Beginning

If I were called on to write a script for a movie featuring parents of deaf children, it might go something like this:

SCENE 1. Two young expectant parents. She, very obviously pregnant, talking about their hopes and dreams for their coming child. The father talks about "him" becoming President; the mother talks about "her" becoming President.

SCENE 2. Birth of a baby boy. Both parents brimming with joy. Mother with a serene, happy expression as she gazes down at baby. Father obviously filled with pride.

SCENE 3. Baby about 3 months of age, in crib, playing with rattle. Mother walks into room and calls to baby. Baby does not turn. Mother frowns.

SCENE 4. Baby in high chair. Mother at kitchen sink behind baby, washing dishes. She drops a platter, which makes a loud noise, and baby does not respond. Mother's frown deepens.

SCENE 5. Baby about 7 months of age. Parents talking at breakfast table:

Father: That was some party we had last night.

Mother: How good our baby is—he did not wake up even

though we made all that noise. . . . Do you think something could be wrong with him?

Father: No! He's perfect in every way!

SCENE 6. Father sneaking up behind baby, who is sitting in high chair. He calls loudly. Baby does not respond. Father picks up drum and bangs it loudly. Baby looks around, sees father, and grins. Father is relieved.

SCENE 7. Father and mother walking with baby, who is now about 1 year of age. Airplane goes by overhead and baby does not respond. Parents look at each other over baby's head with fear and apprehension.

SCENE 8. Later that evening, parents talking in hushed tones:

Mother: I think there is something wrong with him.

Father: I think you are right; do you think he might be retarded?

Mother: Let's talk to the pediatrician.

SCENE 9. In pediatrician's office. Kindly doctor observes baby playing on examining table. Mother and physician talk:

Mother: I think there is something wrong with my child. He does not respond when I call him.

Doctor: (Going behind baby, clapping his hands quite loudly. Baby looks around.) I do not think there is anything wrong. You are just being overly anxious. After all, this is your first child.

SCENE 10. A few months later.

Mother: (Very angrily.) I think something is wrong with our child and I am going to take him to a hearing center.

Father: I agree that we should.

SCENE 11. Parents entering hospital building. Father carrying child; apprehension is etched sharply on both parents' faces.

SCENE 12. Inside sound-proofed room, child seated at table with toys in front of him. Loud piercing sounds are coming from loudspeakers mounted on walls. Child does not respond. Mother huddled in other corner of room behind child, tears streaming down her face.

SCENE 13. In physician's office:

Doctor: I am sorry, but your son is deaf and there is nothing we can do medically to bring his hearing back.

Father: Are you sure there is nothing you can do?

Doctor: Yes.

I do not know if Hollywood would ever be interested in making a movie of such a script. Allowing for all the individual differences, however, it is fairly typical of the experiences of parents as they come to the recognition and ultimate diagnosis of deafness in their child.

The Mourning Reaction

The initial experiences of the parents of a deaf child are fairly predictable and almost universal. Deafness is seldom considered by the parents or the pediatrician because of the low incidence of severe hearing impairment and the hidden nature of the defect. Consequently, few people have sufficient information or experience to even consider deafness as a possibility. Parents at first are blissfully unaware that anything might be wrong with their child. Then one parent, usually the mother, because of her more frequent contact with the child, begins to suspect in a vague way that something might be wrong. Again, it is usually mental retardation, not deafness, that is first suspected. At some point, the mother confides her fears to her husband, who often finds it difficult to accept the fact that anything might be wrong with their child.

The reality begins to close in on both parents and they surreptitiously begin testing the child. For the next period of several months, they live with a great deal of doubt and fear. Part of the difficulty in testing a young infant, particularly if one is a prejudiced observer to begin with, is that the child may legitimately respond to the noise if it is above his hearing threshold (deafness is seldom total and almost all deaf people have some residual hearing), or the child may respond to the vibrations, visual stimuli, or air pressure created by the hitting of the noisemakers and give a pseudoresponse. The scripts in scene 6, where the father gets a response, and scene 9, where the pediatrician also seems to get a response, are very typical of the situation that occurs when the child is between 6 and 12 months of age. During that period the parents are on an "emotional rollercoaster," alternating between periods of despair, when there is no response, and elation, when they obtain a pseudoresponse.

The scene in the pediatrician's office might seem rather harsh; it is, however, fairly typical of parents' reported experiences. In a survey that we conducted [3], we asked more than one hundred families what their initial experience with a physician was like. Almost all families reported consulting the pediatrician first; over 43 percent reported that knowing what they know now, the pediatrician gave them the wrong advice. In many cases, the physician responded in the same way as the father in scene 5—by denying the problem. In other cases, parents reported that the physician said something like, "Yes, he is deaf, but there is nothing you can do until the child is 3 or 4 years of age."

Retrospective studies such as this one are not necessarily accurate, because when the parents try to recall what happened in the pediatrician's office, they are filtering that memory through feelings of fear and anger. Nevertheless, in our survey, we found that most parents consulted the pediatrician when their child was approximately 12 months of age, and that the diagnosis of deafness was made when the child was 18 months of age. That six-month gap between consulting the first professional and the diagnosis of the problem must therefore be caused, in part, by the failure of communication between the parents and the physician.

Ultimately, the parents make their way to the audiological/otological facility, where the diagnosis of deafness is finally confirmed. For many parents, the initial statement "Your child is deaf" brings forth a feeling of relief. For the mother, it is usually "Now somebody finally believes me," or "Thank God, it's not retardation." The parents, in most cases, have been prepared for a year for that diagnosis. The emotionally devastating impact is provided by the otologist when he informs the parents that there is nothing that can be done medically to correct the hearing problem. So far, the consoling support for the parents has been the faith that "they" (professionals) can fix it. After all, "they" send men to the moon and "they" transplant hearts, so surely "they" must have the cure for deafness.

It is when they realize that the child is deaf and *will always be deaf* that parents begin to mourn actively or grieve a monumental loss—the fantasy that their child would be like all other children and might even be President (see scene 1).

The psychological reactions to crisis have been well documented by Shontz [6], and they provide a useful model for understanding the reaction that parents of deaf children experience immediately after they receive the diagnosis. The crisis reaction reported by Shontz is also strikingly similar to the work of Kübler-Ross [2], who studied the emotional reactions of terminally ill patients. There seem to be psychological principles that are almost universal in crisis reactions.

Shock

The state of shock is characterized by a divorcement of oneself from the crisis situation. Shock is usually a short-term state, lasting for a few hours or, at the most, one or two days; it serves as a defense mechanism to get the parents through the initial stage of mourning. The person in shock is in a low-anxiety state and sometimes reports a bemused looking-at-oneself. As one mother said, "I remember being in the doctor's office; it was as if I were on a stage. I remember asking some questions. I don't remember the answers. All I really wanted to do was to go someplace and hide." Parents rarely remember much from that first interview. They will sometimes recall nonessential facts like, "I remember that the audiologist wore a red jumper, but I can't remember her name." Although the parents are present physically, they are not attentive intellectually or emotionally.

Recognition

In the recognition stage, the awfulness of the situation is realized by the parents, and they begin to acknowledge the situation emotionally. "This is really happening to me. I have a deaf child who will never hear at all, who will always be deaf." Active mourning begins at that stage, at which very strong feelings emerge from the parents.

One predominant feeling is that of being totally overwhelmed. I think all parents, at one point or another, feel inadequate to the task of raising their child—whether he is handicapped or not. When the parents are presented with a child who has special needs that they must fulfill, they feel even more overwhelmed and inadequate. That feeling of inadequacy is aided and abetted endlessly by inspirational messages from professionals to the effect that "This child's success is going to depend on you." (I used to give that speech regularly myself.)

Total confusion is another common reaction of parents; it is so easy for professionals to forget how esoteric the terminology of their field is. For example, terms such as decibel, audiogram, and otologist are not familiar to the layperson, and lead to bewilderment when used casually by a professional. The parents, having no background knowledge of deafness, are unable to judge the quality of the information that is being given them by professionals, relatives, and friends. Thus, total confusion results, often leading to a near-panic reaction in parents. In the initial stages, the parents' problem is rarely one of too little information but, rather, of too much given in too short a period of time [5].

Another strong feeling experienced by parents at that time is anger. Anger occurs when there is a violation of expectations. I have never yet met a parent of a deaf child who has not been, at some level, deeply angry. A fundamental anger is directed at the child. "Why did you have to be deaf and, therefore, not meet my expectation for a normal child who would be like everyone else?" This particular anger is rarely acknowledged; more often, it is displaced onto the professional—to the physician who was slow to make the diagnosis, and to the one who was not able to cure the deafness.

The parent's anger is ultimately turned inward and manifests itself as depression. Parents usually find themselves immobilized at that point, having little energy for anything but the barest essentials of living. "All I could do was stay in my room; every time I looked at my child I burst into tears." The lack of energy seems to be a result of the battle to keep the anger suppressed. Anger itself is an energy, and it takes a great deal of determination to keep it from surfacing to consciousness.

Another source of anger is the feeling of impotency and

frustration. Suddenly, as a result of having this handicapped child, the parents have lost control of their lives. Now others —teachers of the deaf, audiologists, and otologists—are making decisions that will alter the parents' lives radically, without the parents having much control over the process. Plans and dreams that parents had may now have to be abandoned. There is also the very helpless and awful feeling that they cannot do anything to make their child better. As a parent, the feeling of not being able to help my children when they are hurting is one of the most devastating feelings I have ever experienced. The feeling of parental impotency is very powerful and leads to a feeling almost of rage, which rarely receives direct expression.

It is not uncommon for parents at this time to want to bargain. Parents have so poignantly said, "If I could only give him my ears, I would gladly do it." The "bargaining" of the parents is very similar to that described by Kübler-Ross concerning the terminally ill patient, who is waiting to bargain both with the doctors and, ultimately, with God. It is a measure of the anguish the parents feel and it cannot be alleviated directly by the professional.

Guilt is another predominant feeling, especially in the mother, who has had the responsibility of carrying the child during pregnancy. Parents have an almost obsessive need to find the "cause" and to affix the blame for their child's handicap. They often engage in the blame game at this point: "If I had not been so wild in my youth, this would not have happened." "If I had taken better care of myself during pregnancy, then this would not have happened." "Your aunt (notice it is never "my" aunt) doesn't hear too well." And so on. Parents can get fixated very easily at this "searching-for-the-cause" stage, and they devote huge amounts of energy and time seeking an answer to the question of causation, which rarely can be answered definitively. Furthermore, even if an answer is forthcoming, it rarely solves anything on an emotional level for the parent.

The feeling of guilt leads to further resentment of the child; and parents may then begin to feel guilty about feeling resentful: "I shouldn't feel this way." They begin to wonder if there might not be something wrong with them for feeling so much resentment toward their own child.

Another frequent manifestation of the guilt feeling is parental overprotection of the child. "Now that one bad thing has happened to you, I am not going to ever let another happen." The parent will frequently "dedicate" her life to making this child the best deaf child in the world. This dedication can exclude everyone else, including the father, and can be very unhealthy for all other family relationships.

The parents also suffer a loss of their sense of invulnerability. Perhaps this can be described best as the loss of trust that the world is a very safe place and that nothing bad is going to happen. Our sense of invulnerability, while perhaps naive, enables us to move freely and to risk (as, for example, in having a child) without thinking too much about consequences. For the parents of a deaf child, life has reared up and smacked them in the face; they will not be able to approach living with quite the same carefree trust they had before they became parents of a handicapped child.

Denial

After the active grieving stage, the parents enter a period of defensive retreat, or denial. This reaction is a coping mechanism, which reduces the extreme anxiety level felt during the recognition stage. Denial can take many forms. One is wishful thinking: "I used to wake up very happy, so sure that the whole thing was just a bad nightmare. I would run into my child's room and try to wake him by calling his name, and, of course, I could not, and it would start all over for me." Wishful thinking is also shown in the search for the miracle cure. Most recently, acupuncture has fulfilled this role for parents. Very often the parents embark on a quest for a more optimistic diagnosis and keep seeking "one more" opinion. There is a very fine line between the "shopping" parent, one who is constantly seeking an optimistic evaluation, and the responsible, accepting parent, who is seeking a confirmation of a previous diagnosis. The "shopping" parent is one who fails to listen to what is said. She will tend only to hear and report back the more optimistic statements. The "nonshopping" parent is one who is not denying the situation and is able to respond to the total message given after the evaluation.

Denial is often manifested in anger directed at the examining physician: "How could he tell my child is deaf? He only looked in his ear for a few moments. Maybe he made a mistake." This is a very frequent complaint of parents; it might behoove physicians to spend more time with both the child and his parents. Although it will not negate the deafness or the denial, a sensitive approach by the doctor might make it easier for parents to accept their child's deafness.

Denial may also take a more subtle form, as in the case of parents who become extremely active in the politics or fund-raising activities for school programs. Superficially, such parents appear to be very "together," as though they have really come to accept their deaf child. In reality, their going out to all those fund-raising meetings and to those organizational groups is a mechanism they are using to avoid dealing with their own child, who is sadly neglected at home.

What distinguishes the denying, activist parent from the healthy, activist parent is the status of her own child. The child of the positively activist parent is well taken care of, whereas the child of the denying parent is slighted. Sometimes, denying parents will effect a "division of labor," e.g., the father will become active, thereby avoiding emotional involvement with his own child, while the mother is left at home to cope alone. This is a very "delicate" family situation for the professional to deal with, because it is very difficult to "fault" the father—even if he is uninvolved with the problem at home—because, after all, he is doing so much for deaf children.

Denial must be treated by both the parents and the professional as a very normal stage in the mourning process. It is also true that parents can become fixated in the denial stage, never advancing to an effective program of habilitation. Denial will be given up as a coping mechanism if the parents can be gently guided to see that there are constructive ways of dealing with the problem of deafness, which can result in a productive, happy child.

Acknowledgment

The next stage of mourning is acknowledgment, or acceptance. At this level, the parent ultimately states: "I have a deaf child and he will always be deaf, and although there is nothing I can do about changing the hearing impairment, there are things I can do to help this child grow into a responsible human being." This is a time of extreme anxiety because the parents must confront reality again. It is a time when the hearing aids are worn on the outside of the child's clothing, and the parents begin to take him on more outside excursions. For me, the best measure of parental acceptance of a deaf child is the condition of the child's hearing aid. The children of parents who are in the denial stage generally will wear their aids underneath their clothing, will have many repair problems or earmold problems, and will frequently go to school without the aid. For the parent, the child's hearing aid is a very powerful symbol of the deafness, and only when the parent accepts the deafness will the problem of dealing with the hearing aid be resolved. The clinician who tries to combat the symptoms of the parent's denial by placing pressure on a parent to have the child go to school with well-functioning hearing aids is doomed to failure. Attention should be directed to the parent's denial; when the parent reaches the stage of acceptance, the problems with the hearing aid will seem to clear up miraculously.

There seems to be a need among parents of deaf children for a public avowal of who they are—in much the same way that alcoholics in an Alcoholics Anonymous (AA) meeting begin by stating their names and then the fact that they are alcoholics. The parents may begin—in a counseling relationship with a professional, then perhaps in group meetings with other parents, and, finally, in general social situations—to talk about their child's deafness freely and openly and, in a sense, come out of the "closet" and emerge as parents of a handicapped child.

Constructive Action

The final stage in the mourning process is constructive action, or adaptation. The parents restructure their life-style and reexamine their value systems at this high-anxiety and high-energy state. Much of that stage is very positive. As one parent put it, "I now feel that I have a purpose, that my values are so much better since we have had this child. I would have been a bored suburban housewife, entertaining myself by going to coffee klatches and bridge games. I now know what is important and my life has a purpose. I never realized how much joy there is in having this child. Every time he says something I swell up with pride and happiness. Each thing he does is such a milestone and we all delight in it." Another parent has said, "Being the parent of an exceptional child is an experience full of pain, sorrow, and sacrifice. It is also an experience full of joy, sensitivity, and love" [4].

I have heard statements like those so many times that I no longer pity parents of a hearing-impaired child. I have come to recognize that the child offers a very rare opportunity for the parents to grow, albeit through much pain and travail. For many parents, the raising of a handicapped child has led to a fundamental changing of values and to an enhancement of living. One parent has said, "I would be the last person in the world to tell anyone that mental retardation is a happy circumstance; yet, when our child was born, if just one person had come to us to tell us that despite our sadness there was hope, that this was not the end of the world, but rather a challenge and a uniting force that could bring out the very best in each member of the family, how much more bearable our grief would have been" [1].

Shock and recognition are relatively short-term stages, rarely lasting more than a few weeks. Denial can be a very long-term stage for some parents and is always faintly present for all parents (in later stages, it is called "hope"), but it need not interfere with constructive action. Acknowledgment and constructive action are life-long stages and are constantly changing as life situations change. Parents go through those stages again and again as they are forced to give up old ways of thinking, for example, when they must change schools, when they must change an educational method because of lack of progress, or when there has been some additional hearing loss in the child. All those experiences can set off a crisis reaction. Rarely, though, is the reaction as deep or as severe as the one following the initial diagnosis.

Parental Expectations

The parent, when the child is very young, goes to the professional with many expectations. Many of those expectations are violated, albeit through no fault of the professional;

nevertheless, as a consequence, the parent experiences a great deal of anger. The professional must be aware of those expectations and prepared to work with the anger, since very often the anger stemming from the violated expectations is displaced onto him.

The major violated expectation that most parents have had is the very reasonable one that they will have a normal child. This expectation seems self-evident, yet it is often not appreciated by both the parents and the professional. Most people enter into parenthood with the assumption that their child will be normal and, of course, beautiful, with a good shot at becoming President. And although some anxiety may be experienced during the pregnancy, it is rarely acknowledged or discussed. When they discover the deafness, a violation of their own sense of invulnerability occurs, to which they respond at first with amazement, and then with anger, directed at their child.

The next expectation is that the professional will take care of them, that is, by repairing the damaged ear or by assuming all the responsibility for educating the deaf child.

There are also a great many expectations concerning the hearing aid. Parents tend to use eyeglasses as an analogy: "If they have a vision problem and wear eyeglasses to see normally, why is it that the child with an auditory problem cannot wear a hearing aid to hear normally?" That expectation occurs despite all the warnings of the audiologist, and it leads to the disappointment-anger syndrome. It is another explanation of the problem that causes the parent to have so much trouble getting the child to school with well-functioning hearing aids. Parents have commented on how much they hated the hearing aids in the early stages because they "failed" to allow the child to hear and therefore advertised his deafness.

The most pervasive and, perhaps deadliest, expectation concerns what the parents expect of themselves and of the child. That expectation is the anticipation that they will conquer the deafness with absolute aplomb and grace, never feeling despair (at least not for long) or anger. They want their family to be a loving and cooperative team, with everyone pulling together to produce a "super" deaf child. They feel that their child, of course, will speak beautifully and go on to become something absolutely remarkable, such as the first deaf astronaut. I have never yet met an idealized family, although I have seen many wonderful people struggling with the problems of being human—which means they *do* despair, they *do* get angry, they *do* make many mistakes, and they *do* fumble around trying to do the best they know how to do.

It is clinically vital to explore all the parents' expectations with them, since all those expectations are doomed to failure: the child was born handicapped. The child will not hear "normally," and the teacher will not take all the responsibility for educating the child (although some make a good try at it); the hearing aids will not cure the deafness, nor is it likely that the child will conquer the handicap totally.

Failed expectations lead to a sequence of anger, followed by rejection, and, finally, ending with despair. When the parent, who expects her deaf child to talk as well as all normally hearing people do, realizes that he is going to talk poorly, she becomes angry again. The new anger is directed at the teacher or the school; it also sometimes gets turned inward onto herself and, ultimately, works its way out onto the child. Frequently, the parent first rejects the program and begins a "shopping" expedition to find the best teacher or cure. Eventually, the child himself experiences the rejection and recognizes in some vague way that *he* is the source of the parent's despair.

Expectations limit perception. The parent who expects her child to talk tends to see the child only in terms of whether he is talking well or not talking well, and she fails to see or accept any other aspects of the child's development. It is important, in discussions of expectations for the child's progress, that the clinician not relate his own limited expectations to the parents. This is, I think, equally as damaging as the "unrealistic" high expectations the parents may have. Rather, the clinician's goal must be to help the parents put expectations aside and learn to deal with themselves and their child on a day-to-day basis. Since that goal is very difficult to accomplish, clinicians need to look first at their own expectations in life for happiness and then at their own functioning before dealing with parents and children. When the clinician learns to accept himself and then the parents, he becomes a role model for the parents, making it easier for them to learn a one-day-at-a-time philosophy. It is imperative that parents accept this philosophy in order to produce a well-functioning family and a well-functioning child.

The Professional's Role

As a young audiologist, I defined my counseling role as one of providing specific information to the parents, and I directed them along a prescribed course of action. Now, I see clearly that the "content" kind of counseling was, for me, a distancing tactic. I thought it was "bad" if parents cried; somehow, I felt vaguely responsible for their tears. After all, it was I who had given them the information that their child was deaf.

Information is clearly not what the parents really want or need during those initial stages. Parents in shock or recognition stages cannot assimilate information because their emotions are very strong at that point, and information only adds to their feelings of confusion and guilt. I learned that, although I gave speeches about hearing aids, schools for the deaf, audiograms, and so forth, none of the material was being comprehended by the parents. On subsequent visits I found that I was being asked questions on material that I had thought had been covered thoroughly before. Information is assimilated most successfully when parents are in the stages of acceptance and constructive action. Although at times it is tempting to hurry the process, I have found that I must be patient.

What parents need in those initial stages is time and space to "feel bad" in an environment in which their feelings are accepted. It was hard for me to see that at first, since I thought I had to earn my fee from the parents by showing them how much I knew. Actually, I was not being helpful at all by distancing the parents from me and from their own feelings. The implication in the parent-clinician relationship was that feeling (that is, crying) was "bad." It is so easy to imply inadvertently to parents that they should not feel negatively. That implication leads parents to readily assume a second layer of guilt about their emotions, which are perfectly normal and understandable. Feelings are neither good nor bad: they are without value. One can judge behavior in terms of whether or not it accomplishes a goal, but feelings just are. Both the professional and the parents need to realize this fact.

Now, during the initial interview with parents, after it has been decided by all of us that the child is hearing impaired, I ask the parents what they need to know. I find, generally, that they will ask a few desultory questions to which I give minimal answers. To the question of how they are feeling, the usual response is "numb." At that point, I give the parents the name and phone number of a parent of an older, hearing-impaired child to visit,* and I set up an appointment for them to return in about a week. During subsequent visits, I find that the parents can talk more openly about their feelings and can assimilate information better.

As a general rule, I seldom volunteer information to parents, because they are not usually ready for information until they begin to ask content questions. Giving information is

* These parents have been through a parent-education course and have had a brief training program to create a parental hot-line. The parent-to-parent contact can be a very effective counseling situation. Empathy and freedom occur in that kind of relationship far more quickly than it might in the parent-professional relationship.

still one of my functions in the relationship, but my speeches are dispersed over many sessions and generally are provided only in response to the parents' questions. If parents fail to question me about something I think they need to know, I will, of course, manage to supply that information. My general "rule of thumb" for this situation is to tell the parents as much as they need to know until our next appointment.

There probably comes a time in the life of every professional when he is asked whether or not he is the parent of a deaf child; it may even be stated in the form of an accusation. For example, "How can you understand my pain when you have never had a handicapped child?" My response to this question is that if we talk about feelings, then we can relate universally. None of the feelings I have described in this chapter are alien to me. I may not have experienced all of them specifically toward one of my own children, but I know what it is like to feel overwhelmed, confused, and angry, and I can relate to those feelings as a human being. As long as my relationship with parents allows us to express our feelings, then we can truly relate as people.

Counseling is not an esoteric skill, but it does take a willingness on the professional's part to share his own feelings and give of himself. As defined and referred to in this book, the counseling relationship is an interpersonal relationship that allows for mutual growth and the expression of feelings as well as facts. The professional must learn to provide the kind of responses and the atmosphere that facilitate the development of an effective counseling relationship.

Summary

The parents' initial stages of awareness that their child is hearing impaired is characterized by increasing doubt and anxiety. After the diagnosis is confirmed, the parents' reactions seem to follow a crisis pattern of shock, active mourning, denial, acceptance, and constructive action. The professional must be very cognizant of the parental expectations as they relate to the rehabilitative process. The professional can facilitate the crisis-reaction process best by adopting a nonjudgmental, listening role, rather than one in which he is a provider of information.

References

1. Canning, C.   "The Gift of Martha." *The Exceptional Parent* 5:9-13, 1975.
2. Kübler-Ross, E.   *On Death and Dying.* New York: Macmillan, 1969.
3. Luterman, D., and Chasin, J.   "The Pediatrician and the Parent of the Deaf Child." *Pediatrics* 45(7):115-116, 1970.
4. Michaelis, C.   "Merry Christmas Jim, and Happy Birthday!" *The Exceptional Parent* 6:6-8, 1976.
5. McDonald, E.   *Understand Those Feelings.* Pittsburgh: Stanwix, 1962.
6. Shontz, F.   "Reactions to Crisis." *Volta Review* 69:405-411, 1967.

2
Counseling the Parent

The issue of deciding where counseling leaves off and conventional psychotherapy begins is a very knotty one, which is beyond the scope of this book. Counseling, when it is not information-based, need not be considered as an overwhelming task by the speech and hearing professional. For the purposes of this book, counseling is defined as a relatively short-term relationship involving people who are in stress situations but are otherwise functioning well in their life situations. The counseling relationship allows and encourages the expression of feelings (affect) and is essentially educational in nature.

Psychotherapy, on the other hand, is a long-term process for people who are not generally functioning well in their lives. Certainly there are considerable areas of overlap and some parents of deaf children have sought psychotherapeutic help after or concomitant with a parent-education program. Very often, the parent's enhanced emotional sensitivity (initiated by having a handicapped child) leads her to realize that she is having marital or other difficulties as well. At that point the parents seek help.

Counseling Approaches

Several approaches to counseling exist, all of which have considerable value to the professional. The approaches vary from being heavily psychiatrically oriented to being educationally oriented; each has a different orientation in terms of the client involved. Those approaches can be classified into four broad areas that might seem very divergent in theory, but in practice there is considerable overlapping.

The Psychoanalytic Model

The psychoanalytic model maintains perhaps the most traditional view of the psychiatrist-patient relationship. Based on Freudian observations and experiences of treating psychosomatically ill patients, it is essentially a medical model in which the patient is viewed as being "sick." This model is most familiar to parents and is most threatening when they perceive themselves as having to deal with a "shrink" (actually, most psychiatrists are "expanders" rather than "shrinkers"). According to the psychoanalytic view, all behavior is motivated by drives and instincts. The subconscious plays an important role in influencing the various defense mechanisms that people use to cope with tension. The counselor works to help the person in therapy recall previously repressed materials, which usually involve some early childhood traumas. By gathering insight into the effects of those traumas on present behaviors, the therapist can help the person to change and grow.

The Behavioral Model

In almost direct contrast to the advocates of the psychoanalytic model, practitioners of the behaviorist model are not concerned with a person's past history. Their therapy is directed instead at the person's present behavior. In that approach, all behavior is viewed as learned, and all changes in behavior and growth are considered to be a direct result of learning. The therapist functions as a learning expert to whom the client describes his present behavior and his desired behavior. For example, the client may be afraid of heights, and he may want the therapist to help him learn to ascend a high building and to look over the top without experiencing any fear. By using successive approximations (moving up one floor at a time) and reinforcement (substituting a good feeling for the anxiety by recalling feelings associated with a happy time), the therapist helps the client to alter the present behavior to the desired behavior. The behavioral approach is essentially an engineering model, in which all behavior and terms are defined operationally. An important concomitant of the behavioral approach is the contract. The behavioral contract is a negotiated agreement between the client and the counselor, in which the desired behavioral changes are specified, with both parties concurring as to their respective areas of responsibility.

The Rational Therapy Model

The rational therapy approach was first articulated clearly by Ellis [1], whose thesis is that the source of interpersonal difficulties lies in the irrational thinking underlying much behavior. Essentially, the approach requires that a scientific method be used to carefully identify the client's problem and then the therapist can proceed in a very logical manner to help the client change his behavior. It is a cognitive, content-oriented approach in which the client takes full responsibility for his own behavior. Very careful attention is paid to the language the client uses in discussing his view of the world. A basic tenet of the rational approach is that one feels as one thinks, and, therefore, altering one's thinking can affect one's feelings.

The Human Potential Model

According to the humanist method, people are viewed as being self-actualizing; that is, they have a basic need to become competent, to grow, and to mature. The potential for growth is within each and every person. Emotional difficulties arise in people who have learned not to value "self" and have ceased to listen and to respond to their own self-actualizing drives, seeking wisdom from outside themselves. A recent book by Sheldon Kopp [3] entitled *If You Meet the Buddha on the Road, Kill Him*, reflects a Zen teaching that the only true Buddha is within oneself. Therefore, if one meets anyone else claiming to be a Buddha, he is false and must be slain. That teaching is the essence of the human potential philosophy, which holds, in effect, that if people are left to their own devices, they will select that which is good for themselves. That opinion contrasts with the other counseling approaches, which suggest that people need considerable help (exploring their past, programming, or modifying their thinking) in order to find "the good." In the humanist approach, the therapist operates as a facilitator and functions to release the self-actualizing (Buddha) drive within his client. *Neurosis* is viewed as a failure to respond to one's self-actualizing drive and, consequently, as a blockage to learning.

All the approaches described herein are effective to a greater or lesser degree. There does not appear to be any *one* preferred method of counseling that works for all clients and for all therapists [2]. The professional needs to select the counseling style and approach that is most congruent with his own personality. The issue of counseling preference is fundamentally an attitudinal one; the way in which the professional views the world and other people within it will determine which counseling approach he selects. I have found the contractual notions of the behaviorists and the language awareness of the rationalists to be valuable clinical tools. For me, however, the client-centered approach of the human potential movement, as articulated by Rogers [5, 6], is most personally congenial.

In the client-centered approach, the relationship that is established between the counselor and client is primary for the client's growth and for the release of his self-actualizing drive. A great deal of caring and trust are engendered in that relationship, which allows for mutual risk-taking that, in turn, produces growth. The established relationship is highly democratic and very much person to person. According to Rogers [5], if the following counselor attributes are developed, changes will evolve in the client.

COUNSELOR GENUINENESS. Sometimes referred to as congruence, *genuineness* is realized when the counselor is basically a whole or integrated person. It is the quality of honesty and the degree to which a professional can be sensitively aware of and accepting of his own feelings without projecting them onto his client. The therapist's genuineness, in terms of his own inner self, is expressed in his sensing of and reporting of his own felt experiences as he interacts in the counselor-client relationship.

UNCONDITIONAL POSITIVE REGARD. Unconditional positive regard is an essential concomitant of the counselor-client relationship, because it allows the client to feel free to explore all issues without fear of losing the counselor's regard by revealing so-called bad things. To have unconditional positive regard for an individual means that one respects the person regardless of the different values that might be placed on her behavior. The counselor accepts the client for what she is, regardless of her behavior. Unconditional positive regard is similar to the feeling that a parent has for her child—that is, she values the child although she may not necessarily be in accord with all his behavior. By projecting unconditional positive regard, the counselor sends a clear message that he cares for and about the client.

EMPATHETIC UNDERSTANDING. Another necessary condition for a good counseling relationship is that the counselor attempt to understand the client's particular frame of reference. The counselor must be willing to listen to the "faint knocking" and to respond sensitively to the client's feelings in a nonjudgmental, reflective manner; he attempts to understand the client *as if* he, the counselor, were the client. Although such depth of understanding is never entirely possible, the counselor must try to grasp the client's particular views and perceptions without judging them as good or bad. The listening aspect of the relationship validates the client; it is a message the counselor sends that says, in effect, "You are very important to me and I want to understand your frame of reference."

Anxiety on the client's part is necessary to provide some motive for change; in the case of the parent of the handicapped child, that anxiety is already present. In addition, the client must perceive the counselor's genuineness, unconditional regard, and empathy so trust can develop in the relationship.

It may not be possible to establish a counseling relationship with all clients. At times I have not been very successful in establishing a healthy working relationship with certain parents, possibly because I was not very congruent or accepting. Also, there have been times when it was very difficult for me to develop a positive regard for a particular parent; that was usually a direct result of some unresolved issue within myself. I find it very difficult, for example, to work with parents who abuse their children physically (I suspect this is because I have not worked through all of my own angry feelings about my children). Only when I can allow myself to hear and respond to the parents' own pain can I begin to develop a positive regard for them. I find that as I resolve increasingly more of my own personal conflicts, I am able to establish more successful counseling relationships with parents. The "failures" are a signal to me of some unresolved personal issue of my own and, as such, are personally enriching.

Implications of the Humanistic Approach
to Counseling Parents

The person-centered counseling approach has many implications for the professional; foremost is the responsibility
placed on him to work with and maintain his own personal
congruence. The professional's personal growth must be
treated as a basic concomitant of training programs and of
continuing education. Just as an audiologist needs to keep
abreast of the latest and most sophisticated hearing assessment instruments, the counselor must constantly learn about
himself as a human being functioning in interpersonal relationships.

Next, the professional must become fully aware of his own
value system and acknowledge that the parents may have different ones. Every attempt must be made to understand what
the differences in value systems are, to respect those differences, and to make the necessary adjustments in the teaching
approach. For example, the minority-group parent does not
trust the "establishment" teacher and has relatively little
faith in the school as a vehicle for positive social change;
rather, school is often seen as a place to indoctrinate the child
and obliterate his cultural background. Such a parent has a
very different orientation from the middle-class parent, who
places a great deal of trust in the establishment and in schooling. The professional needs to appreciate both these differing
value systems and needs to respond to the parents' point of
view, even though it may be alien to his own.

The professional also will have to reexamine his position

as a "helper" in the relationship that he enters in dealing with parents of handicapped children. I am reminded of the following story.

An elderly woman was standing on a busy street corner. A Boy Scout came up to her and crossed her to the other side. A few moments later, another Boy Scout came and crossed her back. She stood on the corner for a while longer, and then another Boy Scout crossed her back. A man watching the proceedings asked her why she was standing on the corner. She replied, "I come here to help out the Boy Scouts."

When one examines the helping relationship, it is not always apparent who is helping whom. As a matter of fact, it is very often the case that the person giving the "help" is actually the recipient, i.e., the Boy Scout. Helping is a very delicate issue in interpersonal relationships, since any time help is given, there is an underlying message of "You are incapable." The Boy Scouts, for example, were telling the elderly woman that she was not capable of crossing busy intersections by herself; if the woman were not self-confident, she could very well have become afraid to cross the street when there were no Boy Scouts around.

The professional working with the parent of a deaf child is also a helper. Moreover, the parents of a deaf child are desperately looking for someone to relieve them of the overwhelming responsibility of managing their child's disability. It is very easy for the professional to assume the responsibility for the parent—i.e., to become the "savior." The savior role occurs very frequently in the helping professions and it seems to have reached epidemic proportions in the field of deaf education. For the professional, it can become a way of enhancing self-esteem: "After all, I cannot be so bad if so many people need me." It seems to me that many therapists enter a helping profession because of an already lowered self-esteem, and then they rapidly establish many very dependent counseling relationships.

The problem with a mutually dependent relationship is that it limits the future growth of both parties. The parents are compelled to manipulate the professional into taking care of them, and the professional needs to keep the parent dependent to continually enhance his own self-esteem. Relationships such as these are a source of a great deal of (often unexpressed) resentment; both the parent and the professional have lost or have given up degrees of personal freedom. The professional feels pressured to serve the parents, to know the answers to all their questions, and to be prepared to make decisions for them. Such a situation is highly burdensome, and, at some psychological level, leads to strong feelings of resentment. The parents, on the other hand, while outwardly very appreciative, are, in fact, constantly pandering to build up the professional; they need to see the professional as omniscient, to rationalize their dependency on him. Subconsciously, however, parents also carry a great deal of resentment. The more "needy" the parent is, the more accentuated her inadequacies seem: "If I really need him, then I must be pretty inadequate." This is a tough message for any ego to take, and it often leads to unexpressed (or indirectly expressed) resentment. Also, when the parent is very dependent, she often feels that she cannot afford to express her anger, since the professional might become angry and withhold his services. Relationships in which anger cannot be expressed are not very satisfactory in the long term to either party involved.

A good gauge of the professional's success is the parent's reaction following the counseling session. A parental response such as, "Why did we come here? I knew all that before I came," indicates that the counseling was probably beneficial. The counselor can judge himself to have been least helpful when the parent leaves thinking that the counselor is wonderful: any time a person has a "hero," it is usually at the price of some self-esteem. To be sure, parents can be appreciative and information can be provided. The important ingredient of the successful counseling experience is the maintenance or enhancement of the parent's self-esteem. Genuine help is given indirectly and does not allow the recipient to lose her self-esteem.

To be most helpful, the professional must learn to enhance his own self-esteem in ways other than by harboring dependent ("savior") relationships with his clients. When the professional is congruent in the Rogerian sense, he has no need for approval or dependency relationships. At the very least, he is aware of his emotional needs and does not allow them to interfere with the client's self-actualizing process. The counseling relationships that work best are those in which the professional feels responsible *to* and not responsible *for* his client; this distinction must be perceived by the parent as well. If the parent maintains responsibility at all times for herself and her own behavior, there will be maximum opportunity for growth.

Counseling Strategies

The most critical influence on the counseling process is the counselor's attitude. The humanistic approach assumes that wisdom resides within the individual; therefore, all techniques of therapy should facilitate a relationship between people that will draw on their innate wisdom. If the relationship is warm and nonjudgmental, and the therapist is congruent and responsive, growth will ensue. With that idea firmly in mind, the professional can address his attention to some specific tools that can be used to enhance the quality of the relationship and facilitate the growth process.

Time

The management of time is a very important element in the counseling situation. A firm contract should be made about the length of each individual session and the number of counseling sessions to be scheduled. I am very firm about the use of time and will not extend a session beyond the contracted time; there is always a specific beginning and termination point to the relationship. The limited amount of time available then serves as an impetus to the parents to work toward solving their problems, especially since it is made clear that I will not do the work for them. In an open-ended commitment, parents might tend to avoid dealing with painful material, thinking that they could get to it at some vague future date. All contacts begin with my being silent and, if the parents choose, nothing needs to be said or done for the entire session. As time passes, counseling sessions invariably get "heavy"; that is, more hidden material and more emotional material gets dealt with toward the end of a session or toward the end of a relationship than in the initial stages, which is partly a result of the time pressure itself. However, openness will not develop unless the other ingredients, trust and caring, have been established.

Contract

The issue of mutual expectations must be dealt with early in the counseling relationship; that is, what the parent expects or wants from the professional, and what the professional expects from the parent must be decided on. Many relationships fail because expectations are implicit and, in addition, are not complementary. For example, a parent who expects a counselor to tell her what to do has very different expectations for the counseling process than does the counselor who is assuming a nondirective stance. If the issue of expectations is not dealt with, the relationship will deteriorate, and anger will develop, although probably it will not be directed at the appropriate source. Therefore, the counselor needs to ask the parent what she wants from him so he can direct the relationship toward those expectations; then they can begin to negotiate a contract.

Basically, a contract determines the duration of the relationship, what it will entail, and its purpose. Contracts do not need to be very detailed or legalistic, but they should be clear to both parties. Although they can be altered as the relationship develops, they should be agreed on mutually and made explicit. It can be devastating to a relationship when one party changes a contract unilaterally and implicitly, or when the expectations of the parties involved are not made explicit.

Language

I have a poster in my office that states, "The shape of my world is the shape of my language." The way in which a person talks to herself reveals her attitudes about the world; for example, someone who seldom uses the "I" form sees herself as always being acted on—as not being the agent of the action —and, therefore, not responsible for her own behavior. I have found it very profitable to pay careful, almost literal attention to the language that parents use. I do not manipulate their language, but I do seek clarification when its usage seems obscure. The following examples may prove helpful to the counselor.

I insist on changing *we* and *us* to *I* and *me,* which forces the parent to take responsibility for herself.

PARENT: We are feeling very uncomfortable with the silence.

ME: Who is uncomfortable with the silence?

I insist on changing *should* to *want to* or *choose to.* Use of the word *should* always creates a deficiency statement—the parent is not taking responsibility for herself and is operating as though some outside agency were responsible for her behavior.

PARENT: I should go back to that audiologist.

ME: Do you want to?

I insist on changing *cannot* to *choose not to* to determine whether this is an external restraint or an internal constraint.

PARENT: I cannot talk to my pediatrician.

ME: Do you choose not to?

I insist on changing *but* to *and* because it reduces ambivalences.

PARENT: I agree with you but . . .

ME: Do you really agree or are you afraid that I will be angry with you?

Use of indefinite pronouns, such as *it* and *them,* may reflect vague thinking. It is good policy for the counselor to request that the parent specify what it is she is talking about.

When language is kept clear and concrete, a great many confusions seem to disappear. Language changing is carried out gently, preferably when not too much emotion-laden material is being dealt with. As the relationship progresses, the parents generally self-correct and even correct the counselor when he makes an error.

Listening for Affect

The listening behavior of the counselor is a vital ingredient of the relationship. Listening validates the speaker; it communicates a sense of worth to him. It implies that "What you have to say is important to me and I want to understand as fully as possible what your internal state might be like." This sentiment is not something that can be faked—at least not for any length of time. One may postulate a continuum of responses the counselor may give to a statement of the parent. That continuum may vary from silence to giving information, providing that the silence of the counselor, for example, can communicate to the parent that he understands what is being said and is permitting the parent to continue talking. By far, some of the best things said in my counseling sessions have been "said" in silence.

The next response in the continuum might be an acceptance remark, such as "Uh huh," which allows the parent to maintain the momentum of the thought while receiving the counselor's acceptance. It is an utterance that says, "I am here and I hear what you are saying."

The counselor can be reflective by paraphrasing the content or the feeling that was communicated without any interpretation or introjection of his own values. Such responses are helpful to the parents in that they enable them to hear, or "see," what they have been saying. For example, the parent might say, "People are so impatient with other people who do not talk well." The counselor's response might be, "It sounds as though you are worried about whether or not people will accept your son."

The clarification response, e.g., "Can you tell me more about that?" asks the parent to delve further into the topic. It is essential that the parent feels she has the option to not answer whenever the counselor asks a question; and that sense of control will diminish her resistance. The question is a very difficult interpersonal communication. It has a tendency to put the person being questioned on the defensive (this is particularly true of any "why" question), and leaves the person wondering if there might not be a "right" answer that she should search for. Therefore, questions need to be worded carefully and used prudently.

Finally, the counselor may wish to provide information. That must be done cautiously when the parent is truly seeking content. As a general "rule of thumb," information should be provided only when the parent shows that she is ready to receive it by asking a content question.

It is possible to classify the questions of the parent into the categories of *content, confirmation,* and *affect.* Content questions are those in which the asker seeks specific information that she assumes is known by the listener. Parents are ready for content when they are in the stages of acceptance and constructive action. Most questions that are not procedural in the initial contacts are either confirmation or affect questions.

Confirmation questions are really pseudoquestions. In that situation, the asker has already taken a particular stand but is unwilling to reveal that position. The question, "Do you like my hat?" is almost surely a confirmation question and must be approached with extreme caution. When one treats confirmation questions as though they were content questions and answers them, one usually ends up putting one's foot in one's mouth. Those questions are best responded to with another question. For example,

PARENT: Is _____ School a good school for the deaf?

COUNSELOR: How did you hear about that school?

The other type of question is the affect question, in which a strong emotion exists that the parent is unwilling to reveal or is unaware of at the time. Rogers refers to those questions as the "faint knocking." For example, the parent might ask, "Do drugs taken during pregnancy cause deafness?" If one dealt with this as a content question, the response would be a long dissertation on the effect of drugs during pregnancy. On the other hand, as a confirmation question, one might respond with, "Did you take any drugs during your pregnancy?" Treating that as an affect question, one could respond, "It must be so easy to feel guilty about having a hearing-impaired child." The affect response can then lead the relationship into sensitive emotional areas, and although that might seem to be a risky response, it usually pays very high dividends in that it gives the parent a chance to examine her guilt feelings. In this case, the affect response usually works better than a confirmation such as "Do you feel guilty?" since the confirmation question tends to activate the parent's defenses, whereas the affect response leads to a feeling of closeness and communion: "Somebody heard me and understands."

None of the given responses is necessarily any better than

any other in a given situation. It may be very appropriate to deal *only* with content in the relationship, or to continually check for confirmation. Mainly, what the counselor does will be a function of the contract. In the initial stages, when the parents' emotions are especially high, very few of their questions are really content questions; most fit into the latter two categories—confirmation and affect. As a general rule, it is more fruitful for the counselor to respond to the affect questions in the initial stages of the relationship, and as the feelings of guilt, anger, inadequacy, and so forth get dealt with and discussed, he may begin to respond with more content. If the counselor responds to the content first, the same question will return to him later in one form or another. It is only when the affect is dealt with that the counseling relationship can progress into content areas.

Confrontation

Fundamentally, confrontation entails pointing out discrepancies in another person's behavior. It is a high-risk response and should be used only after trust in the relationship is well established. For example, the counselor might confront the parent by saying, "You are telling me how angry you are, yet you are smiling, and I am confused." Confrontation always thrusts the relationship into the present and forces a reevaluation of previously accepted material. It brings the person's present behavior into juxtaposition with some formerly stated position. Confrontation is also a validating strategy that sends the message, for example, "You are important enough to me that I wish to get this straight between us." Initiation of confrontation is very critical. The modulated tone of voice that is descriptive, rather than evaluative, will minimize the parent's defenses and allow her to scrutinize her present behavior.

None of the "techniques" described in this section can take the place of the counseling relationship itself. Some of the worst counseling sessions I have had have been when I have consciously tried to use techniques. When I become so self-conscious that I rely on techniques, I lose my genuineness and the relationship does not develop. It is when I lose my sense of self and allow myself to feel part of the situation that my responses are spontaneous and authentic; it is only in retrospect, when I review the session, that I can see the techniques I have used. It is when I operate on my implicit knowledge that I am almost always "right" in the relationship, that is, most facilitative. I fail miserably when I try hard to do the "right thing" in a very conscious, stilted manner.

The beginning counselor will have to spend some time learning and practicing technique. The technique of listening for affect is probably the easiest to teach, though often very difficult to put into practice. Management of the relationship in terms of time and contract is relatively easy to learn. It will take time for the beginning counselor to feel comfortable with heavy emotional material and, in particular, with confrontation situations.

It is important to remember that the counseling relationship can withstand a great deal of stress, as long as the basic caring comes across. In other words, the novice counselor needs to be sure that he really cares for and about the parent; if that sentiment is communicated to the parent, growth will take place. Mayeroff [4] describes a caring person as one who is honest and authentic, has the courage to take risks, and sees the other person as having potentialities and a need to grow. The caring person is one who recognizes his own need to be needed but does not impose his will on the other person in the relationship; he has patience, trust, and hopes for changes and growth. This is a tall order, but every professional counselor who works with parents will need to cultivate the characteristics of the caring person.

The counselor must not be impatient with the development of the relationship; a nondirective approach does require time. The time element of a relationship is so beautifully expressed in *The Little Prince* in his encounter with the Fox that I quote it here:*

"What must I do to tame you?" asked the little prince.

"You must be very patient," replied the fox. First you will sit down at a little distance from me—like that—in the grass. I shall look at you out of the corner of my eye, and you will say nothing. Words are the source of misunderstandings. But you will sit a little closer to me every day . . ."

The next day the little prince came back.

"It would have been better to come back at the same hour," said the fox. "If, for example, you come at four o'clock in the afternoon, then at three o'clock I shall begin to be happy. I shall feel happier and happier as the hour advances. At four o'clock, I shall already be worrying and jumping about. I shall show you how happy I am! But if you come at just any time, I shall never know

* Excerpted from *The Little Prince* by Antoine de Saint-Exupéry, copyright 1943, 1971 by Harcourt Brace Jovanovich, Inc., and William Heinemann Ltd., Publishers, and reprinted with their permission.

at what hour my heart is to be ready to greet you . . ." [pp. 67, 68].

And he went back to meet the fox.

"Goodbye," he said.

"Goodbye," said the fox. "And now here is my secret, a very simple secret: It is only with the heart that one can see rightly; what is essential is invisible to the eye."

"What is essential is invisible to the eye," the little prince repeated, so that he would be sure to remember [p. 70].

Summary

The field of counseling may be divided into four broad areas: traditional, behavioral, cognitive, and human potential. The humanistic, nondirective approach of Rogers can readily be used as a model for the professional dealing with parents of a handicapped child. In that approach, the relationship that is established is paramount to growth. The qualities of congruency, empathetic listening, unconditional regard, and the perception of those qualities by the parent are necessary for the relationship to develop. The techniques of time management, using direct language, listening for affect, and confrontation have been described as tools for the professional; they are not, however, substitutions for the counselor's attitude. Adequate time must be allowed for the relationship to develop, the basic ingredient of which is counselor caring.

References

1. Ellis, A., and Harper, R.   *A New Guide to Rational Living.* Hollywood, Calif.: Wilshire, 1977.
2. Hansen, J., Stevic, R., and Warner, R.   *Counseling Theory and Process* (2nd ed.). Boston: Allyn & Bacon, 1977.
3. Kopp, S.   *If You Meet the Buddha on the Road, Kill Him.* Palo Alto: Science and Behavior Books, 1972.
4. Mayeroff, M.   *On Caring.* New York: Harper & Row, 1971.
5. Rogers, C.   *On Becoming a Person.* Boston: Houghton Mifflin, 1961.
6. Rogers, C.   *On Personal Power.* New York: Delacorte, 1977.

3

Developing Programs for Parents

The major problem in the development and maintenance of educational programs for parents appears to be the administration of them. Many programs, and the professionals working within them, start out with the logical assumption that, since the parents are the most important people in the child's life, professional attention needs to be directed toward them. A parent-centered program, as referred to in this book, is one in which the primary thrust of therapeutic attention is directed toward the parent, as opposed to a child-centered program, in which the major energy is directed toward the child. The two types of programs are not mutually exclusive; parent-centered programs do provide services for the child and child-centered programs do provide services for the parent. The difference lies in where the professional's attention is focused. Both programs have the same goal—of producing a child who functions at his maximum potential. For the purposes of this book, the *parent* is defined as the primary caretaker of the child. In practice, that might be a grandparent, some other blood relative, or a foster parent.

Difficulties in Developing Programs

Three general reasons that developing programs for parents seems to be difficult to accomplish are (1) professional insecurity, (2) the "Annie Sullivan" syndrome, and (3) parents' fears.

Professional Insecurity

Professional training programs rarely provide any information or experience for the student in how to deal with parents. They concentrate instead on providing considerable information and practicum experience with the handicapped child. As a result of that imbalance in emphasis, the young therapist feels very insecure in dealing with parents, who may be older and more experienced in the care of children. So the therapist begins to adopt defensive strategies to "distance" the parents, the most common one being to impart information. The content-based relationship is completely controlled by the teacher and subtly puts the parents down by increasing their feelings of inadequacy. That one-sided way of dealing with parents becomes habitual with time, and older teachers tend to rely on content strategy almost exclusively. In some circles, that approach is considered very professional. It is only when professionals feel secure as people that they can allow more intimacy and more freedom in their relationships with parents.

The "Annie Sullivan" Syndrome

Many teachers of the deaf seem to suffer from the "Annie Sullivan" syndrome; that is, they see themselves as being totally dedicated to the child, who is a "lump of clay" (maybe it is a Pygmalion fantasy). The best example of that fantasy may be found in the play, *The Miracle Worker* [2]. In that play, the parents are depicted as being totally ineffectual and, in fact, contribute to the young Helen Keller's problems considerably. It is only when Annie Sullivan literally takes Helen Keller away from the parents and keeps her under her complete control in a separate cottage that progress is made. Unfortunately, generations of teachers of the deaf have been influenced by that play and its film version. That story also does a poor job on parental confidence, both by pointing out their own ineptness and in setting very high expectations for the children and their teachers; after all, their children are *only* deaf.

Guided by that fantasy, it becomes very difficult for professionals to focus on the parent for any length of time; in fact, the parent (on some psychological level) is seen as an impediment to the realization of the fantasy. If a parent education program is to succeed, the professional must view the parent as the primary recipient of the educational program. It can become very difficult for the professional to work indirectly with the child by working with the parent: after all, how can she get the credit for turning out another Helen Keller if the parent is in the way?

Parents' Fears
Parents also have problems accepting programs focused on themselves: "After all, it's my child who is deaf, not me." Although they may acquiesce to participate in a parent-centered program, their psychological frame of reference is not concentrated on themselves. In the first place, they may be looking for a "savior," someone who will tell them what to

do and relieve them of the burden of having to bring up their handicapped child. Second, they often approach the teacher with all the old fears and strategies they adopted in school when they were children. They have a strong resistance to being back in school and being relegated to the learner (subservient) role again.

Not all parents need nor benefit from a program of parent education. Parent participation is essentially a middle-class value, and since most educators are members of the middle class it is almost universally assumed (within the field) that all parents "should" participate in a program; the parent who does not is somehow "bad" or delinquent. Some minority-group parents, however, do not view schools or, by extension, the teachers, as their saviors, and they do not see the school as an institution to be trusted. Also, some parents fear the school because they view it as being establishment-oriented (since the "establishment" has been active in repressing them, they see the school as an agent of suppression). The schooling of those parents usually has been so bad, and they have so many bad memories of it, that they have no desire to subject their children to a similar experience. That cycle is very difficult to break. The only hope for overcoming it seems to be in upgrading the quality of schools in general.

Moreover, for parents who are wondering where their next meal is coming from or where they are going to live, their child's deafness may be a relatively unimportant issue. That is not to say that those parents are not concerned; it is just that they do not have the energy to deal with the additional problem of their child's handicap. Similarly, middle-class parents who are undergoing severe emotional difficulties concerning, for example, marriage or employment, do not have the emotional resources to engage in a parent-centered program. Therefore, the professional must be careful not to impose the parent-centered program on all parents; parents should be able to choose among programs and to select the one most suited to their own particular needs. The professional must work to ensure that the community, if not his own teaching facility, offers a variety of programs for parents to choose from without imposing any sense that he values one program over another.

Types of Programs

Several varieties of programs attempt to educate parents; their value depends, in large part, on the skills of the professionals involved and their ability to maintain the parent emphasis.

Therapy by Correspondence

In therapy by correspondence, there is no physical contact between the therapist and the parent. The therapist sends a series of lessons to the parent, who returns an evaluation after each lesson in order to receive the next, successive one. For that type of program to be at all successful, excellent written communication skills on the part of both the teacher and the parents are required. Admittedly, correspondence is the least desirable means of conducting therapy, but in situations in which no other professional is currently available or, as a supplement to an ongoing program, it sometimes proves useful. The John Tracy Clinic currently offers that kind of correspondence course [9].

Home Visitation Programs

In home visitation programs, an itinerant teacher visits parents in their homes, usually on a biweekly basis, but sometimes more frequently. That program can be supplemented by parental visits to the center where the teacher is located. Since contact time is so limited, most of those programs are set up to work with the parent. The teacher visits the home and gives a lesson to the child, while the parent observes and, sometimes, the parent gives the lesson while the teacher observes. The teacher and parent then spend some time discussing the lesson and any other concerns the parent may have. The itinerant teacher is often the only professional contact for the parent after the initial diagnosis has been made.

Home visitation programs are implemented in rural or low-population areas that have a large scattering of hearing-impaired children who would have to travel long distances to attend a centrally located facility. One problem with such programs is that the teacher often spends more time on the road than in actual, direct service, and thus she becomes inordinately expensive and services few families. Home visitation can also be very isolating since the teacher and the parents have little access to other professionals, other parents, or both. The teacher needs the backup support of audiologists, psychologists, physicians, and child development professionals that is not available in that kind of program; the parents need the opportunity to share their experiences with other parents who are undergoing an ordeal similar to their own. A tremendous amount of emotional support can be gained from the parent-to-parent contact that the teacher cannot provide alone.

Home visitation programs and correspondence courses are often stop-gap measures to provide families with "something." The problem is that people often forget that, and those programs have a way of becoming permanent. Because some service is being provided, protest is stifled, as is the crisis energy it could generate toward building more comprehensive programs. In the long-term view, the handicapped child would be much better off without those stop-gap measures. However, a home visitation program or a correspondence course can perhaps be effective if it is paired with a short-term intensive program.

Short-Term Intensive Programs

Short-term intensive programs seem highly desirable in rural areas and in conjunction with home visitation programs. Groups of parents and professionals get together for an intensive short-term experience within provided residential facilities. Programming includes parent groups, nursery and tutoring facilities for the children (with active parental participation), information meetings, and psychological, audiological, and medical diagnostic testing of the children. Programs can last anywhere from a few days to two months, and they can be held in summer camp facilities in June or September or on college campuses when the students are not in residence.

One program for deaf children and their parents was the Harmony Hall program [8], which was run in conjunction with Pennsylvania State University. It was a ten-day session, incorporating one weekend, and provided diagnostic testing of deaf children, as well as a heavy emphasis on parent education. The parent component consisted of discussion groups, observations of the nursery, lectures, and formal instruction in direct therapeutic techniques. That program is no longer in existence, probably because of the diminishing rural population of Pennsylvania and the growth of other diagnostic facilities. Recently, a two-week program very similar to the Harmony Hall program was started for the parents of visually handicapped children [3]. The Tracy Clinic in California has for years provided a six-week intensive summer program for parents of deaf children from all over the country.

The short-term intensive program has considerable merit in and of itself, but it would have greater value if it were used in conjunction with a correspondence course or a home visitation program. The itinerant teacher, a professional in the intensive program, could establish a relationship with the parents and with the other professionals in the region. The parents could also make the acquaintance of several other parents and continue to have contact with them after the limited, intensive program was completed. If needed, the program could provide for weekend follow-up meetings and evening meetings to discuss content or provide support on a once-a-month basis.

Demonstration Home Programs

For the demonstration home program, a facility is arranged within the clinic or school to simulate a home. It usually consists of a bedroom, a kitchen, and a bath, all furnished according to general American standards. The parent takes the responsibility of providing lessons within the home situation, under the supervision of the teacher. For example, the teacher and the parent may decide to bake cookies as the day's activity; the parent then supplies the materials and prepares the cookie batter with her child, while the therapist instructs her in how to use the situation to enrich the child's language. The contact also affords the teacher and the parent an opportunity to discuss any issues of mutual concern. That program may suffer from therapist-parent isolation, which is also a shortcoming of the home visitation programs, except that in the demonstration home the teacher can service more families since she has a home base. Also, both the teacher and the parents can consult with a professional staff, which is available at the facility. The federal government has financed several demonstration home projects and several more have been started without federal funds; however, there has been no careful evaluation of the effectiveness of those programs [4, 6].

School-Based Programs

Most school programs are child-centered and operate similarly to the public school system; that is, parents relate to the school through conferences with the teachers, usually twice a year, and through membership in the PTA (Parent-Teacher

Association). Very often, the PTA gets subverted into fund-raising activities and, as a result, a great deal of parent energy gets expended in raising money for the school. Although the parents can learn a great deal from those activities, they rarely result in direct benefit to their own child. Efforts by schools to involve parents more in education are usually sporadic and seldom permanent; their primary mission (as seen by the staff) is child education, with, as a result, energy and commitment rarely being directed to the parents.

Educators in general are aware of the lack of parent participation in schooling and have been trying to rectify the situation. Schools have run parent groups under the auspices of guidance departments and have urged parents to attend classroom sessions [6]. In one innovative program the teachers use cassette recorders to communicate with parents. The teacher records a lesson or instructions for the parents and the parents then make a recording back, thereby communicating by means of the tape carried to and from school by the child [1].

School administrators might want to consider the intensive short-term experience as a way of initiating parent groups and parent contact. From that experience a parent program can emerge as an organic part of the total school program; for example, a family weekend workshop can be a means for convening the staff, children, parents, and administrators in a weekend of lectures, demonstrations, and discussions [10]. More of that kind of school program must be implemented on a fairly regular basis if reaching parents is to be a high priority of the school personnel. The limited contact afforded by the teacher conference or evening meetings is not sufficient to involve the interested parent in the school program.

The major difficulty in the parent-school relationship is the difference in the implicit contracts that each party has in mind. School administrators often think that the contract should call for a great deal of parent participation, although the parents may feel that the school has the expertise and should therefore educate their child. The contracts or expectations of each party must be made explicit, with the obligations of each party clearly spelled out and accepted; for example, both the school personnel and the parents may need to feel that it is permissible to write contracts which outline that the parents need to participate only minimally. The professionals, on the other hand, must be sure that the school-based program is of sufficient magnitude; that is, they must have enough time and control to provide a high-quality, child-centered program. The cruelest deception in current programs occurs when the school is providing only limited contact with both the parent and the child (which is insufficient to provide lasting stimulation for the child). Such programs cannot provide satisfactory habilitation of the child. If programs cannot provide enough contact time to the child on a daily basis, then there must be a significant parent-focused component to counterbalance that deficiency: parent participation should be inversely proportional to the amount of available contact time for the child. That is, programs with limited access to the child must invest more time in the parents, whereas those programs that have more access to the child cannot afford to do enough work with the parents.

Clinic-Based Parent Programs

Clinic-based programs are probably the most difficult to describe since there is so much variety in the types available. Basically, the program is a function of its location and the available community resources. Most clinic programs are begun when a need is perceived in the community, usually by an audiologist, that is not being met by existing educational institutions. Very often, the clinic-based program has a short life, since the educational institutions begin to expand their services to encompass that unique service. Almost all early intervention programs were started as clinic-based programs. The Emerson program was begun as a result of a lack of parental service in the Greater Boston region. That program, begun in 1965, is not offered as "the model" for all programs; each program should be adapted to its own institutional setting and should be consonant with the needs of the community. Many features of the Emerson program, however, are generally applicable to all clinic-based, parent-centered programs.

The Emerson program is available to any parents of a hearing-impaired child between the ages of 18 months and 3 years, who has been diagnosed as having an educationally handicapping hearing loss. Many of those children, especially in recent years, have other disabilities in addition to loss of hearing. The initial contact with the program must be made by the parents; an appointment is then made for them to observe the program. The parent-centered nature of the program is explained, and the parents are given the names of several parents who have been enrolled, as well as a listing of the available child-centered programs in the community, with the suggestion that the parents visit them. Parents are not allowed to make a decision at the initial interview, but they are requested to call us within two weeks if they are still interested. We never do any follow-up; if the parents do not call us, we assume that they have found a more suitable program elsewhere.

No parent has ever been denied admission to the program. Therefore, the parents who are admitted have very carefully selected themselves to participate, and so they commit themselves to a parent program. The contract delineating parent participation is very explicit; over the thirteen years of the program's existence, no parent has failed to complete the year's course.

The facilities of the Emerson program are located within the speech and hearing clinic of a college training program. They include a 20- by 30-foot room (formerly a garage), fully equipped for a nursery school, with a large, one-way vision mirror and a microphone-speaker arrangement, adjoining a comfortably sized observation room. Two smaller therapy rooms with adjacent observation booths are in close proximity to the nursery. A conference room, located elsewhere in the building, is used for the parents' group meetings. The nursery, an autonomous unit within the community speech and hearing clinic, is used to train speech and hearing professionals.

The staff comprises a nursery-school teacher trained in early childhood education and two tutors who, over the years, have represented various backgrounds; for example, we have had speech therapists, audiologists, and teachers of the deaf. Last year we employed (as a tutor) a parent who had been through the program and has a teaching degree. In addition, we have an audiologist and a program director, who also leads the parent group. (The latter is my position; my training is in audiology and education.) I do not select people for the staff solely on the basis of their educational background. I am most interested in selecting people who have good interpersonal skills. I look for people who are caring and who can approach parents with openness and warmth; that is my primary consideration in hiring.

The child and one parent are required to attend the program two mornings each week. The children are placed in the nursery and are given therapy by a tutor assigned to them at the beginning of the year. During one morning session, the parents observe their child in the nursery and in tutoring; during the other session, the parents participate in a group discussion. The program runs for one academic year according to the college calendar. Groups are restricted to no more than eight families with hearing-impaired children.

Over the years, parents have instituted various procedures to facilitate their learning. Each group seems to suggest some new procedure for us to follow and hence each group leaves us a legacy. Within the structure of the program, which meets two mornings a week, we maintain a very flexible stance and allow parents to control their own learning experiences. We have employed all of the following procedures at one time or another.

HEARING CHILDREN AND THEIR PARENTS IN THE NURSERY.
Normally hearing children are placed in the nursery—if possible, a male and a female somewhat younger than the hearing-impaired children. They help differentiate for the staff
and parents between developmental issues and issues that are
due to the deafness. That practice is of particular value to the
parents of deaf children who, even though they have older,
normally hearing children, have a very difficult time determining if a given behavior exhibited by their child is due to
his being two years old or to his being hearing impaired. By
seeing how "deaf" a normally hearing 2-year-old can be, the
parents begin to appreciate the distinctions between the developmental issues and those resulting from the handicap.
In our experience, parents tend to attribute much more of
their child's behavior to his deafness than to his "2-year-old-
ness." The hearing children help the parents and the staff
keep the handicap in perspective. The parents of the normally
hearing children also participate in the discussion groups,
which allows the parents of the deaf children to learn that
many of the problems they are dealing with are human ones
that are not necessarily restricted to parents of children with
special needs. The responses from the parents of the hearing
children have been almost uniformly positive. Those parents
have appreciated the use of the nursery for their children, and
they have all noticed a large increase in vocabulary, which
is attributable to the language stimulation of the nursery staff.
They also feel very enthusiastic about participating in the
parent group; it has often provided them with a chance to

work out some of their life issues as well as to learn about the problems of deafness and of raising a deaf child.

PARENTS IN TUTORING. The program has a strong emphasis on parents as doers, and a few months into the program, the parents begin to administer the individual therapy sessions. We have found it helpful to start the parents off in therapy with a child other than their own. Primarily, that seems to help the parents look at the child objectively, rather than with all the fears and expectations they have built up around their own child. Also, the beginning sessions with their own child are usually disasters. The parents want so much to impress the therapists with how much they know and how well their child can really perform that they enter the situation with a great deal of tension, which is communicated to the child. The child, who has built up a relationship with the therapist by this time, does not want to see his mother while he is with the therapist. Therefore, the lessons seldom succeed at first. Working with another child, the parent has more of a chance of starting off successfully and building her confidence.

PARENTS IN THE NURSERY. After experiencing some comfort in the therapy sessions, the parents are then rotated through the nursery, usually in pairs. The nursery, as opposed to the individual therapy, provides the parents with an opportunity for learning how to stimulate language under natural free-play situations while the children are exploring various media. Parents learn to deal with child management issues under the guidance of a teacher who has been trained in early childhood education. They are encouraged to bring into the nursery various materials that will be used by the children and to begin to explore the use and value of various media as teaching devices.

It is important to note that the therapy and nursery experiences are provided only after a period of guided observation, during which parents have a chance to work through a great deal of their affect and are able to handle content. There must also be a high level of trust among staff and parents. I would be very hesitant to put parents in those situations unless they were well prepared; the chance of failure, at least in the parents' eyes, is great, and this can lower their self-esteem considerably.

EVENING MEETINGS. Parents are expected to attend one evening meeting a month, at which time content is provided by guest speakers. Currently, we at the Emerson program have six evening meetings a year. The first meeting is usually a talk by an otologist on the medical aspects of deafness, with an audiologist discussing audiograms and hearing aids. The second meeting features deaf adults who talk to the parents about their experiences. The third meeting generally features a child-development specialist who discusses the characteristics of the normal 2-year-old child. In subsequent meetings, we sometimes ask parents of older deaf children to discuss how they made their decisions concerning methodology and programs, and sometimes representatives of various schools are invited to talk about their programs. The last meeting is always reserved for program evaluation and "graduation."

The format and content of the meetings are varied, depending on the needs of the group.

SPOUSE MEETINGS. The term *spouse,* as used in this book, almost always refers to fathers, although we have had some fathers go through the program while their wives worked during the nursery's hours. Most parent education is "mother education," which can and does cause a great deal of stress in the family. To combat that stress we instituted spouse meetings on a once-a-month, evening basis. The discussions were designed to be nondirective and to parallel the morning discussion groups of the mothers. Those groups have not worked out well—attendance has tended to fluctuate widely and generally has been low. In large part, that seemed to be a result of the monthly nature of the meetings, which made group cohesion difficult to develop. In addition, the men tended to find it more difficult to open up and share and discuss their feelings in a group situation. Therefore, in recent years we have tried a different format; we encourage both parents to come to the meetings. We have enjoyed more success with that arrangement because the groups tend to be livelier when the women are included. In addition, husband and wife have the opportunity to discuss management issues between themselves.

One year we tried a group that included husbands and wives who were not spouses of each other; that made for a very interesting group experience. The men (I think for the first time) were able to hear the women talk without responding defensively, as usually occurred when their own wives spoke. Similarly, the women were able to listen to the men objectively. The issue of spouse meetings is a very real concern, and we have not yet found a solution that seems satisfactory for all groups.

PARENT DAY OFF. We have found consistently that parents get so preoccupied with their child's deafness that they forget to take care of themselves or to develop other interests or abilities. I think this is ultimately unhealthy for the hearing-impaired child because it can lead to the "martyred mother" syndrome, which can be very devastating for the child as well as for the parent. During the second semester we insist that the parents have one morning a month off: on the non-group morning, mothers alternate between doing therapy and working in the nursery, or they simply enjoy having the morning off. On the morning off, we suggest that they do something for themselves that has nothing to do with deafness. Since several parents take a day off at the same time, they often go shopping together, or sometimes they just have coffee and talk informally.

STAFF MEETINGS. The Emerson nursery staff is composed of two therapists, a nursery school teacher, an audiologist, and the director/group counselor. Staff meetings are held weekly and are a critical feature of the program. They provide the one forum for the staff to share perceptions. A program such as this requires a very close working staff that has a common set of goals. Staff meetings frequently parallel the parents' group meetings, in which staff feelings are shared and the basic attitude and philosophy of the program are maintained.

Over the years, our staff has developed a cohesiveness; all the members work well together, with a great deal of trust and affection.

In addition to professionals our staff includes student speech and hearing therapists who undergo training in the nursery program. The students in training augment the professional staff by functioning as aides in the nursery, observing therapy, and giving therapy on the days when the parents are having discussions. The staff meeting is an important means for training the students because it gives them a chance to share their experiences and to listen to and participate fully with the professionals on the staff.

SIBLING DAY. We reserve one morning a semester for siblings of the deaf children to come in and visit. Those children come into the nursery and participate in the therapy session; they are encouraged by the staff to ask questions and to take part in all activities.

For some groups, we have also held a grandparents day, for which we have invited the grandparents in to ask questions and to visit. The parents are encouraged to bring in visitors on their nursery days throughout the year—in particular, grandparents, but also interested friends and relatives.

Suggestions for Parent Programs

For those professionals engaged in, or wishing to engage in, parent-centered programs, the following suggestions may be helpful.

1. *Respect the heterogeneity of the parents.* Parent groups are notoriously heterogeneous. We have had groups comprised of both parents who have advanced degrees and others who have not graduated from high school. The program must allow for both types of parents to absorb content on their own levels. Counseling sessions in which feelings and attitudes are discussed allow all the parents (together with the group leader) to participate as equals. When the group leader discusses content, he can individualize it by relying on the parents' questions and reading material.

During the first several years of the nursery program we gave workbooks to the parents. Those books consisted of observation guides for nursery and therapy, rules and regulations, a directory of parents and staff, suggested reading lists, a history of the program, and material on maintenance of hearing aids. However, we found that the parents generally did not read the material and frequently forgot to bring it with them to the nursery. The role of the traditional teacher (reminding parents to bring their workbooks) was incompatible with the accepting relationship that we wished to have with the parents. Consequently, we have abandoned the use of workbooks and will only give reading material to parents when they ask for it. We also have a library of books on deafness, and the parents can circulate those books among themselves. Those parents who like to read have that option. Conversely, those who seldom read usually take one book out at the beginning of the semester and return it at the end of the year. We do not put any pressure on the parents to read; they do so if they wish.

2. *Give the parents responsibility for determining their educational program.* Because of the diversity of needs that exists within the parent group and the goal of the education program to produce parents who are assertive and willing to take responsibility for themselves and for their child, the professional must allow the parents maximum freedom to determine their own programs. We have constantly found that parents intuitively know, far better than the professional does, what they need to do in order to maximize their growth. Techniques or procedures evolve from within the parent group. It is also imperative that parents "do"—that is, become active in therapy and in group situations.

3. *Separate the diagnostic function from the parent program.* Almost every group we have worked with has included parents of multiply handicapped children. Those parents originally came into the program on the assumption that their child was only deaf. It is not possible to maintain the nondirective approach and assume a diagnostic, "expert" stance with those parents. We share our concerns about the child with the parents, usually after the parents initiate talking about their fears, and we then refer the family to a diagnostic facility, which is not associated with the parent program. After the parents return from the evaluation, we are in a position to discuss issues with them and to respond to their feelings. In that way, we can maintain our counseling role.

4. *Keep the counseling function carefully integrated with the educational program.* Many programs employ a social worker or psychologist to do parent counseling. Usually that means that the counselor takes the parents off to a separate

facility while the child's educational program continues under the direction of the teaching staff. That kind of program provokes a negative staff attitude, which can be unhealthy for the parents. The teachers within the program, since they have little access to the counselor, adopt a noncounseling attitude; that is, any time the parent begins to show affect, the teacher suggests that she speak to the counselor. That sends the parent a clear message that affect is very threatening and somehow "bad." From the parents' point of view, being sent to a counselor may be similar to an elementary school child's being sent to the principal's office. They often resent being sent to a psychologist or social worker and feel very threatened by those professionals' titles. I do not know how the counselor can be very effective in that situation, either.

In a well-run program, the responsibility for counseling is everyone's, and doing parent counseling is a commitment of the staff. The staff needs to recognize that parents are not emotionally ill because they express strong feelings and frequently cry over having a handicapped child. They are under a great deal of emotional stress and need to be treated with loving concern by everyone. It is ironic that very often the most effective "counseling" is done by the secretaries or the aides, who are not burdened with a false sense of professionalism, and who approach the parent on a person-to-person basis.

The psychologist or social worker can benefit programs by providing staff support, by increasing counseling skills among the staff, and by being prepared to deal with situations that are beyond the scope of the education staff. If programs include a psychologist to provide direct services, such as leading parent groups, then they must incorporate him into regular staff meetings to keep everyone informed about the parents' progress.

5. *Maintain the parent-centered emphasis.* It is very easy to lose sight of the parent-centered aspect of the program, because the children are so very seductive. I have found that the less contact the teachers have with the children and the more direct contact they have with the parents, the easier it is to maintain the program's focus. Staffing should be supplied to the parent first and then to the child. For example, the therapist is always asked to talk about the parent and how she responded to the therapy situation; then the child is discussed. As soon as possible, parents should be encouraged to take part in all program activities, for example, by providing therapy or working within the nursery. That involvement maintains the parent emphasis for the staff. Therapists in our program have sometimes spent a session talking to a parent without seeing the child in formal therapy; and that is accepted by both the parent and therapist.

6. *Use the parents as teachers.* A frequent criticism leveled at programs for parents is that the parents are not therapists and that by having them "give lessons" to their children, they will become either poor parents or poor teachers. I think that criticism is totally unwarranted. All parents are teachers whether they like it or not. A good parent program does not insist that parents provide formal lessons if that is not congenial to the parent-child relationship. What must be understood clearly by both the professional and the parent is

that there is no incompatibility between teaching and parenting. Teaching is part of everyday living, and the parents of the deaf child need to heighten the linguistic and communicative aspects of their everyday lives to meet the special needs of their hearing-impaired child. A good parent program provides parents with information, role models, and experience in good child management techniques to enhance their overall functioning as parents.

7. *Integrate audiology with the educational program.* The parents' initial contacts with the audiologist usually occur very early in the diagnostic process, when their emotions are at their highest peak. The parents are unable to process most of the information being presented to them at that time, not only because of their affect, but also because of their total unfamiliarity with audiological terms. Audiologists often forget how difficult it is for most people to understand terms such as decibel, intensity, and frequency, as well as the mechanics of hearing-aid maintenance. The parents need considerable time and exposure to those terms and to people who are willing to be patient with them before they can really begin to understand what the audiologist is talking about. In our experience, it takes the parents at least one year, with repeated explanations, before they can begin to understand the audiogram. (At that pace, they sometimes become more advanced than students involved in a basic audiology course.) All programs should provide ample opportunities for the parent and the audiologist to meet and discuss audiograms (which parents tend to treat as report cards) and hearing aids. The frequent informal meetings seem to be much more

facilitative than the formal lectures or diagnostic sessions, in which there is usually little time for talking.

8. *Adapt parent programs to the needs of the population and to the structure of the facility in which they are located.* There is no single correct model for parent programs. Professionals who are located in rural areas, where there is a low percentage of hearing-impaired children, will have to adapt programs in a different manner than professionals who are located in large city areas, where there are many potential families of hearing-impaired children to draw on. Professionals working within a public school facility will have a different program structure (by virtue of their being public servants) than will professionals within a private school or clinic. Some facilities can afford to have dual programming; that is, child-centered and parent-centered programs. Others can afford to have only one. It is always a mistake to try and make one program service the needs of all families. I do not think it is possible to provide both a parent-centered and a child-centered program simultaneously—the parent is inevitably short-changed.

Socioeconomic Status and Parent Education

The Emerson program, not by any conscious design, has attracted predominantly middle-class parents. When we have had lower-class parents they have tended to be middle-class seekers—that is, they tend to be very actively aware of their current status and they want to improve themselves through education and by obtaining better jobs. Those middle-class seeking parents generally have worked out well. However, we also have had a few parents from lower socioeconomic classes, whose participation generally has been unsatisfactory in that their attendance was sporadic and they always seemed to be having a family crisis. During group discussions, they tended to be either quiet (seemingly overwhelmed by the better educated parents) or very anecdotal in terms of their contributions to the group. It was very clear to me that their child's deafness, although very important to them, was only one among many other formidable problems they were dealing with. It seemed also that their energy level and general health was far below that of the other (middle-class and middle-class seeking) parents, and that they did not have the stamina to cope with their child's deafness. The professional might easily mistake the poor attendance and quietness of such parents for a lack of concern on their part. However, that is just not true; I have not yet come across parents, who, at some level, were not concerned about their child or at least striving to make things better for him. The seeming indifference on the part of the parents can very easily be only a misinterpretation on the part of the professional, who has failed to listen sensitively, or it can be a result of an overall lack of trust in the relationship.

The passive admission procedure we use in the Emerson program seems to function as a fairly effective screen. Parents who have the energy and a commitment to parent participation will find and follow through on the parent programs. Parents who do not have the energy or commitment generally will seek the child-centered, directive programs. I realize that

I am suggesting that parent programs will continue to be focused mainly on middle-class parents. I think that suggestion is generally true. Parent-centered education is only one vehicle for producing a well-functioning child who happens to be handicapped, and it is not necessarily the "way to go" for all parents. There are also middle-class parents who do not benefit from a parent program. Those parents seem to be unwilling to make a commitment to introspection or are entangled in job-related or marital problems, and thus they have few resources left for coping with their child's deafness. The professional needs to trust the parents to select the best program for themselves, even though there may be some mistakes (perhaps as in the case of the lower-class parents who chose our parent program). The parents will, if permitted, self-adjust and seek more suitable programs for themselves. Each individual parent possesses insight and the professional must not "push" any particular program, but he must ensure that the community or the program offers a variety of options for the parent to select from.

Deaf Parents of Deaf Children

In the thirteen years that Emerson's nursery has been in operation, we have had only one deaf family in our program. I do not know why we have not worked with more, since we are open to that possibility; we just have not received any other referrals. The deaf family was immensely valuable to the parent group. The other parents, all normally hearing, could see firsthand the difficulties that their child would experience, and they could identify with the early childhood experiences related by those parents when they revealed them to the group. They were also immensely valuable to us in organizing an evening program whereby deaf adults could come and speak to the parents. Fortunately, the possible danger that the deaf parents might have assumed an expert stance and might never have gotten a chance to work on their own interpersonal and intrapersonal issues in the parent group was averted.

The Kendall School in Washington, D.C., has recently begun a group program exclusively for deaf parents.* The feeling of that program's counselor is that deaf parents have specific concerns and counseling needs that are different from those of hearing parents; those differences have not yet been described carefully. One may speculate that deaf parents would have very different attitudes toward amplification (probably highly dependent on their own experience and probably not as important to them as to hearing parents), and toward the use of manual communication (again related to their own education), and that they may vary from hearing parents in many of their initial emotional reactions. Deaf parents were sometimes relieved when they were informed that their child was deaf, because they felt they could raise a deaf child better than they could raise a hearing child; that attitude is certainly very different from that of hearing parents. One may also predict that deaf parent groups would have different kinds of issues concerning guilt and confusion than would a group of parents

* McAleer, I., "The parent program at KDES." In-house memo. Kendall Demonstration Elementary School, Washington, D.C., 1978.

of hearing children. The subject of deaf parents is a very promising one for investigation, and I hope that studies of it are currently being undertaken or contemplated.

The Effectiveness of Parent-Centered Programs

The measure of success in any therapeutic program should be evaluated in terms of how well the children involved achieve their potential. Such data are not currently accessible, since we have no accurate measures of what a given child's potential is. Moreover, we cannot really answer the question as to whether a parent-centered program produces better results than a child-centered program does. To do that, we would need to measure the communication skills of carefully matched groups of children, half of whom are enrolled in a child-centered program and half of whom are enrolled in a parent-centered program. However, if we were to attempt to set up such a study, it would have to be assumed that we could discern and measure all the important variables needed to match the two groups (which we cannot). Furthermore, the families involved would be the same, which is decidedly not feasible. Parents who select a parent-centered program immediately differentiate themselves from parents who select a child-centered program, from the point of view of both their socioeconomic status and the presence of other problems in the family. So while one might match parents according to child variables, the very important unmatched family variables will not allow one to draw any definitive conclusions. In addition, to conduct such a study the abilities of all the staff members would have to be equal, which is really impossible to assess, let alone match. The staff that functions well in a child-centered program does not necessarily function well in a parent-centered program, and vice-versa. Moreover, a research study in which we would use the person as his own control cannot be implemented; once we use a particular kind of educational treatment, we change that person, and when we impose another treatment on him, we are dealing with a changed person and, therefore, different variables. Thus, to give a family a child-centered treatment and *then* a family-centered treatment, and to measure growth after each treatment, would not be valid, since the child would be altered after that first educational treatment.

Those professionals who work in parent-centered programs must accept, at face value, the premise that if the parent is helped, the child will also benefit. Measures of the effectiveness of the program can be determined from the parents themselves. The research collected on actual parental change resulting from educational intervention is extremely sketchy and needs exploration very badly. Most studies seem to rely on anecdotal data, while the remainder use attitudinal or informational scales. None of the studies—in any way—has definitely determined that a parent-centered approach yields a "better" parent, let alone a better communicating child, than a child-centered approach.

One reliable measure of a parent program, however, is the degree of participation of the parents in community action programs. Parents seem to progress through three stages: first, concern for themselves; second, concern for their child;

and third, concern for all similarly handicapped children. Another, and not often stated, goal of parent education programs is to mold the activist parent—the parent who will work hard so that all hearing-impaired children will benefit. Parents are a potent community resource; they have skills and knowledge that can be put to good use for servicing the needs of the community. No one works harder for less money than a parent when her child is involved, and a parent program can be a means of developing and channeling her energy. Also, a huge multiplier effect can occur as a result of parent programs in that many more handicapped children in the community can benefit from the activist parent, who has been "trained" in the parent program, than are actually serviced by the program directly. For example, some parents of the Emerson program became very active in the Massachusetts Parents Association for Deaf Children. In rapid order, the parents influenced passage of legislation to make day classes mandatory in any town where there were five or more hearing-impaired children, published a directory of services, conducted a census of deaf children, established early detection legislation that entitled all high-risk children born in the Commonwealth to have a hearing test at the state's expense, created a hot-line program, and established a parent-chaired deaf advisory committee to work with the Department of Education on deaf affairs. It is no accident that deafness is the only disability that has an advisory board and a statewide coordinator within the Department of Education. For one exhilarating year, the parents even became the funding agents for a high school for the deaf; e.g., Massachusetts formerly had none and now has three, mainly through the efforts of parents.

Because deafness is a low-incidence disorder, it receives little attention from the government bureaucrat. Consequently, the deaf child needs a passionate advocate to promote an equitable distribution of government funds. For the deaf child, that responsibility for advocacy falls on the parent. Oddly enough, the parents can move the bureaucracy more effectively than the professional. For one thing, the parent is unpredictable; she is apt to cry, write all sorts of uncomplimentary letters to newspapers or superiors, or march with banners and her handicapped child on the State House to attract publicity. The bureaucrat retaliates by bending just enough to quiet the more vocal parents and by putting the activist parents on an advisory committee and then not listening to their advice.* The parent, though, is still the bureaucrat's natural constituent—she is the one he is pledged to help and she is a potential voter, so there is a very real desire on his part to please her or at least to quiet her.

---

* I realize that I am being very harsh in my assessment of bureaucrats. I would just like to say, at the outset, that some of my best friends are bureaucrats and I have even been known to take one out to lunch. Nevertheless, as a veteran of several advisory committees, I have had an opportunity to watch firsthand the operation of the bureaucrat within his bureaucracy; decisions and programs are frequently implemented with the speed of a racing snail. The responsibility for the decision, or more frequently for the nondecision, is diffused throughout the system so that it is impossible to identify the decision-maker. It is a very frustrating experience to try to make changes and, in all fairness, there are bureaucrats who are equally frustrated. They are the ones who usually wind up being my friends, but that is another book.

The professional, on the other hand, is generally committed to being polite and rational. He lacks the emotional commitment that the parent can bring to the situation. Anything that he might suggest in the way of program development would be received by the bureaucrat with suspicion that the proposal might be self-serving. Although the professional might be cordially received, he is rarely as effective as an assertive, unpredictable, emotional parent. Professionals, then, can enhance their community effectiveness by working with parents; the parent-education program can be the fertile training ground for the community-minded parent and, as such, can become a vital community resource to benefit all handicapped children.

Summary

If program development is to succeed, it must remain focused on the parents. Various possible alternatives include correspondence, home visitation, short-term intensive, demonstration home, clinic-based, and school-based programs. All those programs require a very clear, mutually accepted contract between the professional and the parents as to the degree and extent of their respective participation. Parent participation must be inversely proportional to the professional contact time: those programs that have the most child contact time can have least parent participation. The parent-centered program tends to be oriented to the middle class; therefore, communities need to develop a number of programs for a variety of orientations to provide options for *all* parents. One positive outcome of parent-centered programs is the activist parent who creates far-reaching opportunities for all handicapped children.

References

1. Gantenbein, A.   "Parents Must First Handle Their Responsibility to Their Child." *Volta Review* 75:352-353, 1973.
2. Gibson, W.   *The Miracle Worker.* New York: Knopf, 1957.
3. Grogan, J., and Maron, S.   "Camp Challenge: A Preschool Program for Visually Handicapped Children and Their Parents." *The Exceptional Parent* 6:37-41, 1976.
4. Lowell, E.   *Home teaching for parents of young deaf children.* John Tracy Clinic, Los Angeles, California: U.S. Grant No. 32-14-0000-1014, 1967.
5. Luterman, D.   "A Parent-Centered Program for Preschool Deaf Children." *Volta Review* 69:515-520, 1967.
6. Miller, J.   "A Demonstration Home Training Program for Parents of Preschool Deaf Children." *American Annals of the Deaf* 113(3):630, 1968.
7. Rotter, P.   "A Parents Program in a School for the Deaf." The Lexington School for the Deaf. Education Series, Book VI. Washington, D.C.: The Alexander Graham Bell Association, 1969.
8. Siegenthaler, B., and Doerfler, L.   "Camp Easter Seal Hearing Program for Preschool Hearing Handicapped Children." *The Pennsylvania Medical Journal* 56(6):459-460, 1953.
9. Tracy Correspondence Course for Parents, Los Angeles, California, 1964.
10. White, N.   A Model for Parent Participation: The Family Weekend Workshop. In *Parent-Centered Programs for Young Hearing-Impaired Children,* P. Elwood, W. Johnson, and J. Mandell (Eds.). Maryland: Prince Georges County Public Schools, 1976.

4

The Parent in the Group

The heart of the parent education program is the weekly group meeting. In that setting, it is possible to work successfully with parents without having any contact with their children. In fact, it is often better for the counselor not to be involved with the child so that he can deal with the parents' perceived reality, unswayed by his own perception of the child. In the Emerson program, all formal counseling is done within the group situation. Only on rare occasions will I conduct a formal individual session with a parent, since most of the individual counseling is done on a very informal basis; for example, during a "nursery" day I might casually sit next to a parent, who might then begin to discuss some things of concern to her.

I have a very strong preference for the group experience for the following reasons.

1. *The group meets fundamental personal needs.* Shutz [4] has postulated three basic human interpersonal needs: inclusion, control, and affection. By *inclusion,* he means the need to be viewed as a distinct person and to have feelings of being important to the group and feelings of personal worth. The *control* need is implicit in the desire to make decisions regarding one's welfare; it connotes a feeling of personal power. Loss of control in the early stages of diagnosis is what leads to so much of the anger that is seen in parents. The need for

affection refers to the close emotional feeling between people; it is fulfilled by feeling lovable.

The group can be a powerful vehicle for having the individual members work through their unfulfilled needs for inclusion, control, and affection. By communicating in an open, accepting manner with the other individuals involved, the group members can allow each other to give up their defenses and to explore more interpersonally fruitful ways of dealing with other people. Rogers [3], in commenting on the use of groups, said,

> But what is the psychological need that draws people into encounter groups? I believe it is a hunger for something the person does not find in his work environment, in his church, certainly not in his school or college, and sadly enough, not even in modern family life. It is a hunger for relationships which are close and real, in which feelings and emotions can be spontaneously expressed without first being carefully censored or bottled up; where deep experiences—disappointments and joys—can be shared; where new ways of behaving can be risked and tried out; where, in a word, he approaches the state where all is known and all accepted, and thus further growth becomes possible. This seems to be the overpowering hunger which he hopes to satisfy through his experiences in an encounter group [p. 11].

Both Shutz and Rogers are speaking about individuals who have specifically contracted for personal growth experiences and who thus convene in an encounter group. The parents of the handicapped child have no such consciously contractual obligation and are frequently "put off" by the notion of a group experience. Some parents go through the initial doubts and then later discover that the group has become an extremely valuable resource for them; others never reach the point at which they can accept the group.

The group becomes a powerful tool for helping the parents through their various stages of mourning and is particularly valuable for the stages of acceptance and constructive action. Generally, it is the first setting in which the parents make a public admission of their child's handicap; the group also functions as the place where, as Rogers [3] said, "new ways of behaving can be risked and tried out." That sense of freedom is vital for the parent beginning the phase of constructive action. Those parents who were formerly withdrawn can see what it is like to assert themselves; those parents who are afraid of being rejected can experiment with confrontation; and those parents who have needed to control situations can learn to give up manipulation and to explore less aggressive types of behavior. The group can often be a very powerful resource for promoting the personal growth of its individual members. In fact, over the past few years I have focused much more on personal growth issues rather than on issues related specifically to deafness. I am not sure whether that modification reflects some inner personal needs of my own or not. However, I find that as the parents gain confidence in themselves, they are much more able to manage their lives in general, and to deal with their "special lives" as parents of a handicapped child with more confidence and ability. Content specifically related to deafness seems to take care of itself.

2. *The group is "wiser" than any individual member.* The group as a whole has more wisdom than does any one individual. Frequently, members of the group will go to the aid of a

member in distress in a very sensitive and spontaneous manner, and without any apparent self-consciousness. Rogers [3] has said,

One of the most fascinating aspects of any intensive group experience is to observe the manner in which a number of the group members show a natural and spontaneous capacity for dealing in a helpful, facilitating, and therapeutic fashion with the pain and suffering of others [p. 21].

Very often, it seems, the least likely member of the group demonstrates the most interpersonal wisdom without being able to articulate it in the least. I always delight when that happens, and I feel an immense sense of relief that I don't have to take all of the responsibility for the group.

3. *The group is an important vehicle for building self-confidence.* For the professional counselor, the issue of helping is a very cogent one. The parents come to him for help, and generally they receive it (perhaps more than they really want). It is very difficult for the counselor, however, to provide help in a way that does not diminish the self-esteem of the "helpee." The group, guided through nondirective leadership, serves as a self-helping experience for the parents; within it, they can operate as helpers to each other and share their experiences and solutions with each other. At any given time, a parent may be in the position to be a helper as well as to be the person being helped. Peer instruction is a marvelous mechanism whereby parents can enhance their own self-esteem. They can accept help from others more easily when

they feel that, at another time, they may be the providers of help.

4. *The group is a vehicle for sharing feelings.* One of the major problems that a parent faces regarding her negative feelings of anger and guilt is that she has little opportunity to share those feelings and to have them accepted. So many people (including themselves) are telling parents that they should not feel guilty or angry. Consequently, the parents frequently add on another layer of affect—that is, feeling guilty about their feelings of anger. However, when they can open themselves up within a group experience and share those feelings they will hear other parents say, "I feel that way, too." Then they exude an almost palpable sense of relief. That sharing of the anger and guilt about having a deaf child is something that I, as a professional, cannot give to parents; it is something that must occur on a parent-to-parent basis. The group becomes the means for that exchange to occur.

5. *The group is an efficient vehicle for processing information.* Because the group includes more people than an individual counseling situation does, it allows for a more efficient processing of content. The source of the content is not necessarily the group leader; in fact, most content emerges from the parents themselves or as a result of questions they ask. Within the group, parents learn to make decisions about what information they need to know and how to seek appropriate sources from which to get it. Those sources can include the professionals within the program, guest speakers, or reading material.

Techniques for Facilitating Groups

The Facilitator's Attitude

A group is very much like an individual in that it develops its own personality and style; and each member contributes to that character, even the seldom-speaking members. Furthermore, in the same way that no two individuals are exactly alike, no two groups are ever the same. The facilitator of the group must learn to accept each group as it is and not try to make it into something else. If a group is not accepted by the facilitator, then his manipulations and disappointments become very apparent, and the group tends to develop behaviors that are not facilitative to personal growth. The group becomes defensive and tries to justify its present behavior or it tries to please the leader by becoming what it thinks he wants it to become. In neither case can there be collective or personal growth.

My nonacceptance of a particular group almost invariably occurs after I have worked with a very open and sharing one. When I begin to work with the newer group, my likely expectation is that they will be like the previous one; I forget how long it took for that first group to become open and sharing. Thus, I must constantly remind myself to go into new groups without expectations for their performance—to just accept the group as it is. I am frequently asked (usually by the parents), "Don't you get bored in a group?" (One response to that question might be, "Are you afraid I might leave?")

I am seldom bored by a group. Although the content of all

group discussions is similar (child management, grandparents, physicians, and so forth), the character of each group is different and the way in which each group deals with interpersonal issues is infinitely varied. For the facilitator, the major problem is a matter of dealing with the growth process—of seeing how the group can grow and allowing psychological space for everyone to learn from each other—and helping to sustain a nurturing environment. Metaphorically, I perceive the group as a confluence of the various life streams of its individual members. While the group is together, there is a comingling of its collective waters, and then gradually each stream branches off on its own, carrying with it some of the water from the other life streams. I merge with the parents for a limited part of our respective life journeys, yet I am able to enrich myself from the pool created by the various groups I have worked with. How can one be bored with that?

Establishing Facilitative Group Norms

The attitudes established in the first sessions become the group norms, and it is very difficult to change a group norm once it has been instituted. Norms are the rules by which a group decides to function; with nondirective leadership, the norms arise implicitly from group consensus. In one group, for example, in which a good, healthy ambience had never developed, a mother complained about the smoking that took place during the first session. She complained that she was allergic to smoke and asked if the smokers in the group (of which there were several) would refrain from smoking or smoke very little during the sessions. The group discussed that suggestion briefly and very politely, although there seemed to be some unexpressed anger beneath the politeness. The smokers, without any formal group decision, continued to smoke. The two implicit norms of the group then became (1) not to be concerned about the welfare of individual members, and (2) not to express hostility directly. Both those norms naturally work very strongly against the development of good group cohesiveness. That group never did develop into a well-functioning unit with a high degree of trust or intimacy, despite my efforts in later sessions to try to resolve the issue and to establish more facilitative norms; the group had already made its adjustment and did not want to open itself to confrontation.

The facilitator probably has no more important function than to help the group establish its own cooperative norms. That task in no way contradicts the nondirective philosophy; the norms do not dictate the content of an individual's contribution to the group and the group is free to reject any norm they oppose. Nondirective group leaders do not walk into a group with a list of already-prepared norms. The most typical way for the facilitator to establish constructive norms is by role modeling and by gently requesting members to behave in certain ways. For example, by initiating a group without taking control, the facilitator has shown that he intends to be a nonauthoritarian leader. At times, the facilitator will have to be more explicit in working to get a norm established, particularly concerning the language that is used during the meetings (for example, getting the individual members to use the "I" form). Occasionally, groups may develop implicit nonfacilitative norms, at which times the group leader would probably want to comment, for example, "This group seems to be operating on a 'let's be nice to everyone' basis." That remark gives the group a chance to discuss its norms; it may very well decide to continue to operate on the "let's be nice" basis, in which case the leader must accept that norm for the group.

Acceptance of Feelings

Whenever a feeling is being expressed by a parent, the facilitator must be sure that his response is one of total acceptance, so as to create a climate within the group in which all the participants feel psychologically safe. It is very important that the participants feel they will not be judged by the leader or by the other participants. Parents are often very ashamed of some of their feelings; frequently they will begin by saying, "I know I should not feel this way, but I am very angry at my child." That statement is a very critical juncture in the group; the speaker is testing the climate to see if it is advisable to reveal her anger. When that happens, there is a kind of collective drawing-in of breath, and an immense sense of relief is exhibited within the group when the statement is accepted by everyone. Other parents can then begin to share their own angry feelings and to receive support from the group. At some later point, the group needs to talk about the "should/ought" quality of feelings and to discuss the notion that feelings just *are* and do not have to be valued as "good" or "bad."

Language

From the beginning, I insist that the participants in the group "own" all their statements. I gently but firmly reject statements that include terms such as some people, we, and society, which are used to avoid personal responsibility. I insist that the person speaking use the "I" form. In addition, other words that are examined carefully are should, but, and cannot (see pp. 36–37).

Here and Now

The facilitator needs to bring a sense of immediacy to what a participant is talking about: "Some people make me very angry," might aptly get the response of, "Is there someone here you are angry at?" The parent can then take that opportunity to deal with some issue that she has within the group. It is always more helpful when the discussion is centered on material that everyone has access to, so that the members can give information and receive feedback. The more immediate the experience is, the more exciting it is. Nothing is more deadly for the group than the participant who narrates anecdotes that are limited to his own experience; in such a case, the interest level in the group diminishes rapidly.

Checking Out

A fundamental interpersonal communication skill that is important in the group situation is checking out the reality with another person. Many of the problems in interpersonal relationships are a result of assumptions that a person makes without bothering to "check it out"; for example, the parent who feels that I might be angry with her because I did not smile when I saw her could operate on that assumption for a long time—to the detriment of our relationship. If she could check out that assumption, she might find that I did not smile because a tooth was bothering me; she might also find that I was angry with her, and we would then have a chance to work that anger out. If checking-out behavior is well established in a group, I invariably relax; I know that my behavior and statements will not be misunderstood because the participants, if they are confused, have agreed to test the reality by questioning me. Checking out is a fundamental group skill; without it, groups seldom develop and, instead, the members operate on their own individual fantasy levels, allowing widespread untested assumptions to run rampant.

Respect for the Individual

In the same way that feelings need to be accepted by the group, individual members themselves need to be accepted by the other group members. Each member must feel free to express and to share feelings and information and must feel valued by the group. Moreover, if the group is going to adopt some specific course of action, each member must feel that her individual needs are being considered. The smoking issue mentioned previously was a defeat for the whole group, not just the allergic mother who complained about it: each member "learned" that the other members were not necessarily going to care about her needs. That discovery diminished the trust level among the members to a point at which the group could no longer function effectively.

Authority Norms

Often, the group facilitator is viewed as a father figure who "will take care of the group." It is important that the facilitator not take responsibility *for* the group but that he be a responsive and responsible member *of* the group; rather than setting the rules for the group, he must negotiate with it as to which guidelines are most helpful to operate under. The facilitator should not be responsible for the content of the meetings but he should be willing to share his knowledge. In the process of learning to deal with their own (and other members') problems, the parents have an opportunity to deal with the fundamental issues of becoming truly mature. Growth is facilitated when the individual parents take full responsibility for themselves and all their needs and recognize that, as Kopp has stated, ". . . for the adult there are no mothers and fathers, only brothers and sisters" [1: p. 188].

Another, perhaps more fanciful, way of seeing the facilitator's role in the group is as that of a navigator, who steers and keeps the group on course, with the fuel for the journey being supplied by the group itself. In the beginning, the group usually expects the facilitator to function as the captain, issuing orders, with themselves as the crew, awaiting instructions and then executing them. When the orders are not forthcoming, the "crew" usually becomes very restive and begins to threaten mutiny. Finding that there is no one to mutiny against—that there are "just us plain sea people" on the journey together—they become angry and anxious. Then, finally, they begin "rowing," which allows the facilitator to become the navigator.

Credibility

The beginning stages of the group are also characterized by the establishment of credibility. All participants need time and space to tell their stories and to establish their credentials for being members of the group. Invariably, a few parents tell medical "horror stories" to describe how badly they were treated by some physician along the line. It usually takes several sessions for credibility to be established and for the parents to sort out who everyone in the group is. If the leader is not careful, he can become very insensitive to that initial confusion, since he already knows the identities of everyone involved. The parents also need time to sort out the physical arrangements as well as the scheduling commitments of the group.

The leader's credibility is also a major issue for the group to deal with; parents frequently want to know about my background and they are decidedly relieved to find out that I am not a psychologist. That relief stems from their own fears that something is "wrong" with them that requires the services of a psychologist. Actual credibility evolves as a function of how the leader conducts himself during the sessions; when he appears to them as a responsive human being who is in control and who cares about them, the necessity for all titles and degrees disappear. That evolution, too, takes time.

Groups also become inclusive very rapidly and there is usually a great deal of professed affection and unity. For that reason, we do not allow new parents to join after the second or third session. New parents would find it very hard to "break into" an established group, to have to learn what the operative norms are, and to establish their own credibility. Also, the group would be held back until the new member caught up, and the group's trust level would need to be reestablished.

The initial group unity and affection is extended to the staff, which is very frequently praised by the parents. (I discount that initial reaction, although I bask in the honeymoon nature of that time.) The praise seems to be a function of a lack of confidence in the parents themselves. The parents, at that point, are saying, "The staff and the other parents have to be competent because I'm not." Rarely have the parents any basis for their feeling of staff competency, since they generally have little experience with other therapists or group leaders before enrolling in the program. The parents' praise is a matter of reassuring themselves that they have made the right choice by coming into the program. Later on, the group-staff relationship usually becomes more difficult because anger can and does get expressed; thus, it becomes more honest, and the affection expressed is more genuine. (I can only begin to trust a person's yes's when I have heard her no's.)

Process of Group Development

Each group session usually begins with a discussion of trivial material, and it is very tempting for the facilitator to get impatient and push the group into something "relevant." The group usually gets into emotion-laden material toward the end of the session, as the time begins to diminish. The initial trivia seems to be needed as a way of feeling things out and establishing the fact that everyone is "there." The emotional material that comes out at the end of the session is a function of the realization that there is very limited time in which to deal with the material, and the rush is on. Occasionally, groups will start out with deeply felt material on their own because some member is in a great deal of psychic pain.

Dealing with Silences

Silence will often fall on the group, and it is critical for the group leader to know how to manage it. Four distinct silences can be distinguished.

The Embarrassed Silence

The embarrassed silence is the one that is dreaded socially: "Who will fill the space and start talking?" Most professionals fear the embarrassed silence more than any other; it is the one they tend to fill with content because they have the expectation, as do the parents, that *they* are responsible for the group's momentum and that, if a group is stuck, *they* should get it moving again. It is very critical that the facilitator not break that type of silence; were he to do so with any degree of frequency he would be sending the message to the group that he will take responsibility for filling in all the silences. Furthermore, the vacuum created by the leader's not filling the silences seems to generate the parents to action; it tends to be a mobilizing force for the quieter participants, who then have a chance to get their issues before the group. The parents need time to learn that the leader will not call on them and that if they wish to remain silent and on the periphery, their right to do so will be respected. For some parents, the thought of being "outside" becomes intolerable (inclusion needs) and they use that space afforded by the silence to begin talking. A parent once said, "I get the feeling sometimes as though there is a big lump of time out there on the table and when it gets silent, it just fritters away and I get very anxious. At times, I get angry at you for not speaking and telling me things. I realize now that if I want something to happen here I have to act, and that is a good thing for me." Embarrassed silences tend to diminish over the lifespan of a group; they are very prevalent during the initial meeting and almost nonexistent as the group develops intimacy.

The Changing Topic Silence

The changing topic silence is a pause in which the group is waiting to see if anything more needs to be said on the previous topic. It is a looking-around to determine that everyone is finished speaking. The group leader may use that silence to bring up a topic of concern, although it is best to do that after the group realizes that that interjection does not equate with his taking responsibility for filling the silences.

The Reflective Silence

The reflective silence occurs after someone has dealt with emotionally laden material that the other group members can identify with. It is a time-out to think and to experience the emotions that have been brought to the fore. I have a sign in my conference room (in which the group discussions take place) which states, "Often the deepest feelings are expressed in silence." The reflective silence is a very heavy, palpable feeling in the group, and it takes a great effort to break it. Frequently, group sessions end on that silence, and feelings generated by it are processed or talked about on another day.

The Termination Silence

Sometimes groups announce that they are finished by lapsing into silence toward the end of the session. That kind of silence is useful for the leader to recognize and to use for the purpose of termination. Occasionally, I have not read that silence well and have thought it was just a pause before changing topics. However, I have learned to check out with groups on those occasions to determine if they are finished, if that silence occurs at some point near the agreed-on hour for terminating.

Participation in the Group

Participation within the Emerson group is voluntary, although at the beginning of the program the parents do not always realize that. All group participation should be voluntary. Some parents—in particular, those who seem to have made an accommodation to their particular life-style and do not want to examine their life choices—find the group very stressful. Parents may request to spend the conference day working in the nursery or with the tutors while the group meeting goes on without them. The group leader should not "give permission" for them to leave; it is necessary for those parents to learn to ask permission of themselves. They also need to feel free to return to the group when they wish. Most parents do return after a few sessions away: the pull of the group is very powerful. Although there is no conscious coercion, it is very difficult for parents to resist the value gained in being with the other parents. Some parents occasionally just need time away from the group.

On the other hand, some parents have wished to relate to the program just by increasing their skills specifically concerning the management of the hearing-impaired child, and they do not want to delve into issues of personal growth at all. Groups seem to work best with individuals who have some commitment to introspection; that is, some willingness to examine their lives and to share their insights with the group as they begin instituting some changes. Other parents stay with the group, yet give little evidence of any introspective growth. They contribute little to the discussion, and when they do, it is anecdotal in nature. They probably stay because they never tested their own limits in terms of the issues that were on their minds. The program, and the group sessions in particular, might be equated with setting a table for the parents and inviting them to partake of a meal. Some parents have enormous appetites and eat heartily; others eat scantily; some eat quickly and the leader may not even be aware that they are eating; and some have good manners and others do not. Parents have different tastes and different diets. A professional has to be sure that he has set a good table that is potentially nourishing to all; parents who do not have a commitment to introspection but who do have a commitment to parent education have a place in a parent-centered program and they should have the right to attend the group or not, as they wish.

Stages of Group Development

The Group at Inception

The typical Emerson group consists of eight mothers of hearing-impaired children (occasionally, there is a father present for the day and sometimes he is a permanent member of the group), two mothers of normally hearing children, a few students in training, and myself. Groups have varied in size from five to as many as twelve members, including the facilitator. Groups with more than twelve members limit the amount of space each member can have, whereas groups with fewer than five members lack the "critical mass" necessary for interactions to take place among the members. The group starts out by having the members introduce themselves and describe their children. When it is my turn, I give my full name (without title) and then say something like, "I suspect we are going to get to know each other quite well during the year. I hope we will all find this a place in which we can talk freely."

Then I stop, and usually a very embarrassed silence follows. Parents who have reminisced with me about their opening sessions have frequently commented on how angry they were with me at that time. It is not uncommon for a parent to come to the first session with paper and a pencil, fully prepared to take notes. When that expectation is violated, the parent becomes very angry—although that anger is almost never expressed in those initial sessions. A first-time exchange after a long silence might go something like this:

PARENT A: What are we supposed to be doing here?

ME: It must be hard not having any structure to deal with.

PARENT A: Yes, I don't want to waste my time here when I could be downstairs helping my child.

ME: You are feeling a strong urgency to get down to work.

PARENT A: Yes, I want someone to tell me what to do to take care of my child.

PARENT B: How often should a parent work with her child?

ME: It must be so hard to know if you are doing enough.

PARENT B: I feel so inadequate at times.

With that, we are off to the races, usually dealing with the predominant anxiety that the parents feel about their ability to cope with the problem and to do the necessary job. Anxiety is usually the first strong feeling to emerge from the group.

In the beginning sessions the parents usually ask a great many questions, many of which are posed as confirmation questions, since that type of question carries a very low risk. They do not ordinarily require the parents to reveal much about themselves. Initially, the trust level in the group is not very high, so the easiest way for an individual to "test the water" is to begin asking questions.

At inception, the leader should be concerned with responding to the affect in the group. For example, the parent who asks, "What is the reading level of deaf children when they leave school?" might get the response, "You sound worried about your child's future." That is an open invitation to talk about the anxiety level that is usually very high in parents at the initial stage. When the anxiety level is reduced, the leader can respond to the content. Rarely, though, will it be necessary to answer the parent by giving the data; it is far preferable to give the parents some reading material that contains the answers to their questions. It is very clear to me how little information parents can process in the initial stages; it is only when feelings are dealt with that information can and should be provided.

The Group at Midpoint

At some point (each group varies markedly in the timing), anger emerges in the group. Often, the anger takes the form of a complaint about the nursery: "Why don't we have more structure in the nursery?" However, sometimes it is focused on the therapists. Recently, we had a group that felt one therapist was superior to another, and as a result of having the "poorer" therapist, half of the parents felt cheated. Occasionally, anger is directed at the leader: for example, "Why don't you answer any of my questions?" or, "Why don't you lecture in here?" The emergence of the anger is a signal that the group is at midpoint. The parents are feeling comfortable in the program and with themselves; it is only reasonably secure people who can dare to express anger.

It is hard for many people to deal with anger; it gets confused with loss of love. (For example, I do not believe on a gut level that someone can be angry with me and still love me, even though I know intellectually that I usually love *most* the people at whom I get the angriest.) In early groups, because of my fear of the parents' anger, little or no anger was expressed. I see now that there were many statements that I never consciously perceived as being expressions of anger, to which I generally responded in a defensive way. I was very adept at preventing the anger from emerging directly; for example, the parent who might remark on how dirty the meeting room was would get a response about how hard it was to get good cleaning help in the college, and there would be no opportunity to explore the anger issues. Nevertheless, the anger remained, although defused, and it generally poisoned the relationship.

The biggest source of group failure for me has been unexpressed anger. If a group is to succeed in establishing a high degree of intimacy and in allowing its individual members maximum opportunity for growth, then the group must negotiate its anger successfully, and the group members must find creative mechanisms for recognizing and dealing with it. The group that had the smoking issue could not handle anger. The parents continued to smoke, but they felt angry and resentful toward the allergic mother; she, on the other hand, sat through the meetings, opening windows and looking pained, and she frequently called on me to lecture. She was telling me and the group how angry she was at not having her needs respected. I also was angry at the group, both for smoking me out and for not respecting the allergic mother's rights; I never expressed that anger to the group, either. Instead I told them, "This is the group's decision and I would like you to come to some agreement." I know now that there was no way the group could come to an agreement unless I, as a member, also contributed; my throwing the responsibility for the decision back to them was a reflection of my own anger. In retrospect, it would have been much more facilitative had I expressed my anger openly, thereby letting everyone deal with it. Instead, the group learned how to suppress the anger while maintaining a "nice" and pleasant superficiality. (I was a marvelous role model for them.)

Treating the anger issue provides access to other very important issues. It allows the group to get at the anger that the parents feel toward their children, and the anger that they feel toward being in a dependent position—it is the anger of impotency. Once that fact is recognized, the parents can begin to take action and to mature as self-initiating adults. So, although my adrenalin begins to flow and my anxiety level increases when I hear the first rumblings of anger, I know that that is a critical time and a golden opportunity for the group.

Another signal that the group is out of the inception phase is when they set about trying to define me. That usually evolves from a discussion about what they will call me. I always introduce myself by my first and second names, omitting all titles. Initially, parents append the title "Dr." to my name—mainly, I think, for their own security. It is always interesting for me to watch the parents begin to "work me out"; first they do not use any name (some become very adept at getting in front of me before they begin to talk), and then finally they call me by my first name. However, usually that is done with some trepidation and following some group discussion. Parents frequently revert back to addressing my title when they are experiencing difficulty, and their use of my title often becomes a sensitive barometer of the parents' anxiety level.

Oddly enough, it is when parents stop calling me "Doctor" that I know it is time to deal with more content in the group. Somehow, I feel that the parents are much more evaluative and willing to reject content when David talks than when Dr. Luterman expounds. When David is a member of the group, more information flows freely. As their interest and ability to absorb content increases, parents will occasionally invite guests (such as hearing-aid dealers, parents of older deaf children, and deaf adults) to the meetings. However, there are not too many invited guests, since the groups generally prefer to be unobserved.

At that point too, I become much more willing to share my own personal problems. In the past I had been loathe to do that because I thought it was somehow not "professional"; I have, however, found sharing to be not only personally helpful, but also very facilitative for the group. It helps the group to deal with the authority issue, and it enhances the parents' self-esteem when they can be of help to me. In addition, if I am troubled by personal issues, I do not listen well and I am much less effective within the group; at those times the group members, in turn, very often will assume that I am troubled or angry at their behavior. Although the results of my sharing have generally been very satisfactory, I am still cautious about sharing myself with parents in the early stages of the group, because I feel that at that time they need me to be strong and very much the "Doctor."

A typical group session in the middle phase might go something like this:

PARENT A: I can't get my husband not to dirty up my floors. Every time I wash them, he walks across them with his dirty boots.

(One of the parents in the group begins discussing various prophylactic approaches, such as putting down a rug or mat after washing the floors. None of those suggestions seem acceptable.)

ME: It sounds like he might be angry at you.

PARENT A: Yes, I think he is.

ME: What do you think he might be angry at you for?

PARENT A: (With a laugh.) For having a deaf child.

ME: It must be so easy to feel guilty about having borne a deaf child.

PARENT A: (Crying now.) Yes, I feel very guilty, and then I let my husband intimidate me because I feel guilty.

ME: What else do you do because you feel guilty?

PARENT A: Yesterday I took B. and went shopping and didn't tell him where I was going; he was very angry when I got home.

ME: It sounds like you're very angry at him, too.

PARENT A: Yes, I am!

ME: It also sounds like you are both being indirect about your anger—with him dirtying your floors and you not telling him where you are . . .

PARENT A: Yes.

The group then begins to discuss their own indirect expression of anger and also how unproductive the anger is for their relationships. After a while, I am able to ask the group if they have also felt angry with their children. At that point, several of the parents begin to talk about the anger and resentment that they had felt for a long time but had never expressed to anyone.

PARENT B: I remember feeling so angry at him that I kept saying to him, "Why did you have to be deaf?"

PARENT C: I just didn't want to have anything to do with him—in fact, I didn't even want to be with him. My mother had to come and take care of him for several days.

PARENT D: I felt that way, too. At times, I still feel that way. When I think that he might not talk well and sometimes when I see those hearing aids, I almost want to scream, "Why can't you be like other kids?" (Pause.) I guess what I mean is, why can't I be like other mothers and have normal problems?

MOTHER OF A HEARING CHILD: I get angry at S., too. She's not deaf, but there are times when I wish I weren't a parent, when I feel so alone and tied down.

ME: What do you do with the anger?

PARENT A: (Laugh.) Take it out on my husband.

ME: My sense of you is that you probably take it out mostly on yourself.

PARENT A: You're right.

PARENT D: That's how I feel toward L.; it's good to be able to talk about it to people without feeling ashamed. I'm angry at society, too. Why is it that we spend so much money on arms and all sorts of silly things, and we don't spend very much on helping deaf children? I want to make things better and I get so angry at people who allow deaf children to be cheated.

The group then begins discussing ways in which they could actively improve conditions for all deaf children.

The Group at Termination

The signal that a group is ready to terminate is when the anxiety level becomes very high. Perls [2] has remarked that anxiety is experienced when you leave the *now*. That happens in the group when the parents begin to wonder about next year or ponder, "What will I do without this group?" Groups tend to mourn their demise once the parents realize that their group is terminal. When the mourning reaction for the group takes hold, parents frequently try to bargain again: "Can't we extend the group two more sessions since we had two snow days?" They get depressed and angry, until they finally accept the fact that the group must terminate. They fre-

quently console themselves with the thought that it can continue to live on in them through what they have gained from
the group. Toward the end, groups usually become very intense because the parents rush to disclose material they had
been holding back all year. They realize that they had better
get to work and take advantage of the group setting, so
highly emotional material frequently comes to the fore. Occasionally, a parent who has been very quiet during the year
will take that time (almost always it is during the last session) to vent hostile feelings that she had kept hidden for
the whole year. I have very mixed feelings in that situation; I
usually become angry at the parent and might say, "Why did
you wait so long to tell us how you felt?" Then I realize that
I am angry at myself for failing to be sensitive to that parent's
emotional state and for not being skillful enough to have gotten to that material sooner; I also feel very sad for all the lost
opportunities. I generally share my sadness and anger with
the parent and hope that we will have some other chance to
relate in a more open manner. Invariably, that parent's last-
minute venting of hostility leaves a negative impression with
everyone. I do not know of any sure way of preventing that
from happening again, although I have become more alert
and have tried to solicit feedback sooner from the quieter
members of groups that have followed. Now, if a parent is a
noncontributing member of the group, I will ask her if there
is anything she wants to say. It is sometimes helpful to share
your discomfort with the parent by stating, "I do not know
what is going on inside you and I wish you would share some
with me." That approach has sometimes helped a parent to

express her negative feelings earlier than the final session, so we can deal with her issues before it is too late. That awareness seems to have been fortuitous, because I have not encountered the situation of last-minute venting of anger in recent years.

By the terminal stage, the norms in a well-functioning, well-facilitated group have been firmly established and understood by all. Support is generated by all members of the group and the affection in the group becomes readily apparent. At that point, I begin to feel truly part of the group and generally give up even the faintest responsibility *for* the feelings of others. I relax more despite the anxiety and, usually, a great deal of laughter occurs. The silences that fall within the group at that stage are reflective and companionable; there are no more embarrassed silences. Frequently, groups will prefer the nature of those silences and so the silences increase.

Groups always terminate with loose ends, with some work not yet accomplished. When I first started counseling, I used to think that we could "tie it all together" at the end into a nice, neat package; I know now that that is impossible. A parent once asked, "What are we going to talk about all year? Aren't we going to run out of things to talk about?" Groups never run out of material; a group is really a process, and, as with its individual members, it is always in a state of becoming. There always will be newly emerging material. The group process is much like the peeling of an onion, in that we keep getting to deeper and deeper layers.

The topics that a group discusses usually become apparent in the first few sessions. The issues of feelings, management of the child, husband-wife issues, grandparents, relationships with professionals, and personal growth considerations are the predominant concerns. Groups keep returning to those topics, with noncontributing members of the first go-round sometimes contributing material, or with other members gaining increased insight. The ending is always unnatural and arbitrary; it is determined by the calendar and not by the needs of the group. Groups, however, will fill the available space; they have an intuitive knowledge of what can be accomplished, and they tend to wind themselves down as the arbitrary closing date approaches.

I have not yet found a really completely successful way to help terminate a group; for me, it is a very painful process since I have usually developed a great deal of affection and caring for all the members by the end. My pain is the price I pay for having developed the intimate relationships and I do not begrudge it, although I sometimes forget that contract I have made. I generally terminate groups by telling them,

This is our last session together. I have experienced a lot of groups and, invariably, after leaving a group, I say, "I wish I had said that to that person." I would like us all now to take a minute to think about what we would like to say, and let's deliver the messages in person.

After some minutes' silence, the members begin to deliver their messages, and the group terminates in that fashion. I still get some "I should have saids . . . ," but I am getting much better at delivering the messages.

After the group terminates, I find myself mourning the

loss of it and I am usually depressed for several days. I have learned that I must allow myself the luxury of mourning the loss of a group.

Summary

The group is seen as an important vehicle for the sharing of feelings, for mutual support, and for the processing of content. In order to facilitate a group, the attitude of the leader needs to be without expectation—accepting a group as it presents itself. Norms of acceptance of feelings, acceptance of individuals, here and now, responsibility for all statements, checking out, and not seeing the facilitator as the authority figure are vital for the establishment of a working group. The group at inception is characterized by the development of credibility and inclusiveness as a means of developing trust. At midpoint, anger emerges, along with content questions. At termination, group anxiety is high and much emotionally laden material is dealt with; the group also requires time for mourning its demise.

References

1. Kopp, S. *If You Meet the Buddha on the Road, Kill Him!* Palo Alto: Science and Behavior Books, 1972.
2. Perls, F. *Gestalt Therapy Verbatim.* Lafayette: California Real People Press, 1969.
3. Rogers, C. *On Encounter Groups.* New York: Harper & Row, 1970.
4. Shutz, C. *Here Comes Everybody.* New York: Harper & Row, 1972.

5

Structured Group Experiences

Although content is, and should be, a very important component of the educational program for both parents and professionals, we, as professionals, must also concern ourselves with altering our attitudes. It is not enough for the young professional to leave graduate school full of information; his interpersonal skills must also be well developed. Similarly, an educational program for parents must not give them merely content information about deafness and community resources; it must also allow them to express their attitudes and feelings about professionals and their own children. Parents also need to learn confrontation skills so they can develop the self-confidence necessary to assert their needs. The group experience is immensely helpful to parents seeking to express and change their attitudes.

The group experience can include both general discussion and structured experiences. *Structured experiences*—planned group activities initiated by a leader for facilitative purposes—can be used to supplement the general discussion and to open up a group so its members can release some of their inhibitions. However, the facilitator must exercise caution when using any technique in a group, for he can sometimes inadvertently push a group into deeper intimacy than its members may be ready for. That action, in turn, can leave a group very dependent on the leader to "come up" with something to get them "unstuck." It is very hard to break that dependency on technique, because groups sometimes use it as an excuse for their behavior.

Structured experiences are an organic part of the group experience and, if used judiciously, can be very facilitative. They cannot, however, substitute for a sensitive group leader. In general, structured experiences seem to work best in the short-term workshop situation in which there is a limited amount of time available. Three kinds of structured experiences are role playing, discussion of hypothetical families, and guided fantasy.

Role Playing

Engaging in role playing helps a group to loosen up; it enables the participants to say things that they may have always wanted to say, without having to take immediate responsibility for saying it; for example, a "mother" can allow herself to be very angry at the "audiologist" in ways that she has not allowed herself to be in a real situation. Role playing is also a tremendous aid for increasing the sensitivity of one group for the "other side"; that is, by reversing roles and having the parents play audiologists and the audiologists play parents, each side will learn to empathize with the other.

For that activity, the group is divided into pairs. Each pair role plays privately and then reports back to the group. Sometimes I will divide a group into triads and designate one member as the observer, who has the responsibility of reporting back to the other two members on what she observed. When I do that, I generally prefer to have more than one structured role-playing activity and to have members rotate through the various formats. Groups usually start out feeling very tense, with the members needing time to get "into" their roles. Many of the role-playing situations are conflict situations, and when the sound level in the room gets to a certain point, I know that the group members are "into" their roles. At times, role playing will occur spontaneously in a group. For example, when a mother is reporting that she is very fearful of talking to her family physician, I may offer to play the role of the physician so she can practice on me. Sometimes I will suggest that she play the physician, which is very interesting and usually very informative for everyone in the group. The spontaneous role-playing situations are almost always successful and I much prefer them to the formal, structured experiences.

I have used the following role-playing situations with success both in groups of professionals and in mixed groups of parents and professionals. I give each participant a description of his role only; then I allow each person a few minutes to read her role, select a partner, and go off somewhere to play out the script. Partners do not share their scripts before role playing; afterward, they usually read each other's part and discuss how well it was played. The individual role-playing situations are then discussed in the total group.

Role-playing situations are rather easy to write; interested readers should feel free to use the ones outlined here or to write their own.

Parent-Audiologist Role Play

PARENT: You are the parent of a 6-year-old deaf child. You want very much for your child to be like other children. She had been enrolled in a nursery for the deaf, but you felt that the other children were too abnormal; in addition, your daughter was beginning to "talk with her hands" and you wanted no part of that. You have been taking her to a tutor for the past several years, and you have now enrolled her in a normal nursery school. The tutor has been encouraging you and feels strongly that your child can "make it in the hearing world." You are very angry with professionals in general who, you feel, seem to underestimate your child's abilities. Your child has a vocabulary of perhaps 100 words, many of which are intelligible only to you. You have been told by several audiologists that your child should be in a school for the deaf, but you do not accept that opinion. Recently, you tried to enroll your child in a public school kindergarten class, but the principal and the teacher have expressed fears about accepting your daughter. They have requested further examinations and, on receipt of the reports, they will make a decision. Now you have taken your child to another audiologist and want to know her opinion.

AUDIOLOGIST: You are the audiologist who has just examined the 6-year-old child. You have found a very profound loss of hearing combined with minimal communication skills. The child is using one-word sentences, many of which are unintelligible to you. She responds appropriately when you gesture to her. In your opinion, there is no way this child can integrate in a public school class. The mother, whom you are about to counsel, is concerned about school placement for her daughter.

Husband-Wife Role Play

HUSBAND: You are an engineer. You are used to dealing with facts and with fairly well-defined solutions to problems. You have a difficult time dealing with emotions and emotional issues. You want simple answers to sometimes very complex questions. Crying and other forms of emotionality are difficult for you to accept. You have been extremely busy and very worried about a current project at your job.

WIFE: You have just returned from an audiological evaluation of your 2-year-old child. The audiologist has confirmed your fears that your child is deaf. You have not, up to that point, confided your fears to your husband, who has been extremely busy and worried about work-related issues. You must now *confront* your husband to seek some emotional support.

Teacher-Parent Role Play—School for the Deaf

TEACHER OF THE DEAF: You have a child in your class who is not doing very well. Your school is an oral school and is very proud of its oral tradition. That child has limited oral skills and he does not appear to be a good lip-reader. His language level is poor and he is just not keeping up with the other children in the class. You have spoken to his former teacher, who has told you that his mother is "very difficult" to deal with. Nevertheless, you schedule a meeting with the child's mother with the intention of suggesting that she transfer her child out of the school.

PARENT: You are the parent of a 7-year-old deaf child. You have sent your child to a very fine oral school with the expectation that he would learn to talk. You do not want your child to talk with his hands. You have done everything that has been asked of you by audiologists, teachers of the deaf, and so forth. You feel defensive about your child because you are aware that his speech and language are not very good, but you feel that they are a lot better than the school admits. You feel that he has not had the right teaching. You have been asked to attend a parent-teacher conference.

Teacher-Parent Role Play—Public School

TEACHER: You are a third-grade teacher and you know very little about deaf children. A hearing-impaired child has been placed in your class and your general reaction has been one of panic. The principal has responded to the Individualized Education Program (IEP), which calls for mainstreaming the child without consulting you. The speech therapist has little experience with hearing-impaired children and the tutor assigned to him knows even less about deafness. In desperation, you call on the child's parents.

PARENT: Your 8-year-old child has been integrated into the public school for the first time, at your insistence. He was previously in a school for the deaf and you felt he was *far* superior to the other children there and that he was not being stimulated. At the IEP meeting with the professionals, you made the case for mainstreaming; they planned to integrate your child with the support of a speech therapist and a tutor. He is, however, the only hearing-impaired child in the school and you are frightened at the boldness of your decision. The teacher has called you in for a meeting.

Hypothetical Families

The hypothetical families are fictionalized case studies, usually designed to illuminate a particular problem. I will select a case study for a particular group when I sense that it represents a very cogent issue for the group, or for some members of the group, to help them discuss a specific topic. Hypothetical families were very helpful for me in my early work with groups, when I needed the comfort of more structure and direction in my role as the leader. I seldom use them now because I have found that I prefer a much more unstructured experience. However, I do use them occasionally in very short-term groups or in groups that are particularly inhibited.

The case studies seem to work well for opening up a group. Usually, the group will begin by discussing the hypothetical family in a third-person sense, but very soon they begin to relate to the family in terms of their own experiences. It takes very little time before the group begins to identify with the hypothetical family. Generally, I have given out a written sheet about the family to the group, but occasionally I will just tell the group about that family. In one program, professionals have "dramatized" the families' situations on tape and have played a recording of it to the parent group. That method also seems to be an effective way of initiating a group discussion. I have also used case studies with good results in professional groups.

The first ten of the following case studies have been reprinted from an article in *The Volta Review* [1]. The last five were added recently. Interested readers may use any of them, or they may write their own to suit the needs of a particular group.

1. Mrs. A. is very confused. She has taken her 2½-year-old child, who is neither talking nor seeming to respond to sound, to several physicians. Her family pediatrician has told her that he thought her child was deaf but that nothing could be done until he was 4 years of age. One physician has told her that he thinks the child is mentally retarded. Her husband and her in-laws, on the other hand, feel that there is nothing wrong with the child and that he will "outgrow it." They tell her about an uncle who did not begin talking until he was 4 years of age and who is now perfectly normal. What should Mrs. A. do?

2. Mrs. B. sometimes says to herself, "Why did this happen to me?" She has said, "I know I shouldn't feel this way, but I really resent having a deaf child. He takes so much of my energy and time. He is so difficult for me to control; I worry about him so much. Every now and then, I find myself wishing for a moment that I had never had him, and then I feel guilty about feeling that way. I also

hate to go out with him because of his screaming and because of the stares of passersby when they see his hearing aid. I just can't stand the questions of strangers and their well-meaning advice any longer." What can be done about those feelings?

3. Mrs. C. feels that her deaf child was given to her because of her past "sins." She has devoted herself to taking care of her child. She no longer goes out socially and has dropped most of her friends. She spends a good part of the day working with her deaf child and taking him to his therapy lessons; she spends evenings reading and talking about deafness. She does not trust any baby-sitters. Mr. C. has begun to complain about feeling neglected and he says he is concerned about the two older children, who have not received much attention from their mother. What are your feelings about that family?

4. Mr. D. is a physician, whose father and grandfather were also doctors. He has always wanted to have a son who would be a physician, too. Since he has learned that his only child is deaf and, therefore, will never be able to be a physician, Mr. D. has not devoted much attention to the boy. He has said, "I had so many plans for him. Every time I see the hearing aid it reminds me that he won't be what I would like him to be, and it's really very hard for me to be with him. I know I shouldn't feel that way and it probably is harmful to him, but having a deaf son is a very big disappointment to me." What can that father do?

5. Mr. and Mrs. E. have three children. Their youngest is a

2-year-old deaf child; the other two are 6 and 10 years of age. The E.'s have been very busy taking the 2-year-old to various clinics for evaluations, and they have begun a twice-weekly therapy program and lessons at home. The middle child has responded to his younger brother's problem very well, and, in fact, seems more understanding of it than the oldest boy. The oldest child has reacted with a great deal of jealousy. He is extremely difficult to manage; he throws violent tantrums and often simply withdraws for fairly long periods of time. Mr. E. has reacted to that behavior with stiff disciplinary measures. Mrs. E's reactions have varied from anger to pleading and bribing. At the same time, she recognizes that neither she nor her husband is handling the 10-year-old child effectively. What might they do?

6. Mr. and Mrs. F. have a 2-year-old deaf son. Mrs. F.'s parents live very near them, and Mrs. Z. has not accepted the fact that her grandson is deaf and will "never" be able to hear. She keeps sending her daughter articles from newspapers and magazines about operations and cures for deafness. She is constantly urging her daughter to take him to "one more doctor." Mrs. F. says, "It is hard enough for us to accept our child's deafness, but it is especially difficult when we keep having to explain it over and over again to other people, who don't really listen to us." Mr. F.'s parents, on the other hand, live farther away and see their grandchild rather infrequently. When they do see their grandson, they feel he should not

be punished—"After all, he is deaf." They become upset if either Mr. or Mrs. F. disciplines the deaf child in their presence. How could that family help to reduce some of those conflicts?

7. Timothy G. is a 3½-year-old deaf child with no siblings. He is not permitted outside the house unless accompanied by one of his parents, despite the fact that he lives on a quiet, suburban street. His mother is very concerned that he might be hit by a child on a bicycle, or hit by a car, because he cannot hear. The parents are also afraid that he might fall down and hurt his ear or his hearing aid. Consequently, he seldom leaves his home or plays with children his own age. Should that situation be altered? Why? Why not? If so, what suggestions would you make to those parents?

8. Mr. and Mrs. H. live in a medium-sized town, forty miles from Boston. They have lived in the town all their lives; the father owns and operates a small business there. The parents own their home in the community and they are both very active in community affairs. They have three children, aged 10, 8, and 5, the youngest of whom is deaf and has been accepted in a school for the deaf in a suburb near Boston. Because of the distance involved, the school will accept the child only on a residential basis. Rather than have her daughter board at the school, Mrs. H. wants to move to a community close to the school so that her daughter can attend on a daily basis. Mr. H. is opposed to such a move; he feels that moving to the new

community would disrupt the whole family. What should that family do?

9. Mr. and Mrs. I. find themselves at complete odds over the management of their deaf 3-year-old son. Mrs. I. is convinced of the worth of the aural-oral approach and is trying to teach her son to lip-read and communicate orally. Mr. I., on the other hand, is convinced that only a very small percentage of deaf persons ever attain reasonable oral communication skills. He would prefer that his son learn manual communication, so he can at least communicate easily with other deaf persons. Mr. I. is around his children very seldom, but whenever he is, he uses manual signs to communicate with his deaf son. What can those parents do?

10. Mr. and Mrs. J. have a 3-year-old deaf child. The family lives on an island and, because of the lack of facilities and professional help, Mrs. J. has had the sole responsibility of teaching her daughter. The child is doing well; she lip-reads about 30 words at a time, responds very well on contextual cues, and can use about 15 words expressively. Mrs. J. has placed her child in a nursery school with hearing children, where she also does well; she has just been told that her daughter can begin attending a school for the deaf on the mainland, which means that the child can only get home every 4 to 6 weeks. What should she do?

11. Mr. and Mrs. K. have recently divorced. Mrs. K. has retained custody of their 3-year-old hearing-impaired son.

The court has given Mr. K. permission to visit the child once a week. Mrs. K. finds that her ex-husband's visits are very unsettling to both her and their son. She feels that her son cannot understand why his father leaves and is not home during the week; the child is very confused by the whole situation. Mr. K. also brings a great many presents when he comes, and he takes the child to exciting places; by contrast, Mrs. K. feels that she looks very "bad" to the child and she is upset at the unfairness of the arrangement. What can that family do to relieve some of the tensions?

12. Mr. and Mrs. L. recently attended an IEP meeting at which the presiding educators unanimously voiced the opinion that their 3-year-old child should go to the local school for the deaf. However, that school only offers a program in total communication. The child has been attending an oral-aural nursery school and has been doing quite well in developing his speech and language skills. The parents want him to continue in the aural mode and would like their child to attend a hearing nursery and receive tutorial help. They feel that the educators are suggesting the school for the deaf because it is expedient and not because it is the best facility for their child. The first IEP meeting ended in a deadlock, and all parties agreed to meet again in two weeks. What strategies should the parents employ for the next meeting?

13. Mr. and Mrs. M. have recently found out that their 2-year-old child is deaf. They have one other, older child

who hears normally. Mrs. M. has a deaf brother and a deaf uncle; consequently, she feels somehow responsible for her child's deafness. Mr. M. has not been helpful. He also blames Mrs. M. for causing the child's deafness and has left all the responsibility for the child's education to her. On one level, Mrs. M. deeply resents having that responsibility; on another level, she accepts it as her "punishment." What can Mrs. M. do to alter the unhealthy home situation?

14. The 11-year-old deaf child of Mr. and Mrs. N. is deeply resentful of being deaf. He is constantly questioning Mr. N. about why he is deaf and refuses to believe that he will not outgrow his deafness. He is currently being mainstreamed and is doing quite well academically; however, he has few friends among the hearing children and he does not want to have anything to do with other deaf people. What can Mr. and Mrs. N. do to help their son?

15. Mr. and Mrs. O. are a couple in their 30s who have recently adopted an 18-month-old child, only to discover that the child is deaf and might be multiply handicapped. The adoption is not yet official and the parents have the choice of returning the child to the agency and going on the waiting list for another child. Mrs. O. wants to keep the child because she has grown attached to him and feels that she can be a good parent of a handicapped child. Mr. O. believes that they should return the child to the agency before they get any more attached. He feels that being a parent is hard enough and that being the parent

of a handicapped child is asking for too much trouble. He is not sure he has the resources to be a good parent to that child, and Mrs. O. feels she cannot raise the child without the full support of her husband. What can that family do?

The Guided Fantasy

The guided fantasy technique is highly potent and must be used very judiciously, if at all, by the inexperienced facilitator. Its use will open up a group rapidly and increase the affect level dramatically. It must be planned so it fits into the overall design of the workshop, and ample time must be allowed for the members to process the experience. I would not use that technique with a group unless the trust and intimacy levels were already very high. As with all structured experiences, each individual participant must feel perfectly free not to participate if she so desires, without group or leader pressure for conformity.

I prefer that the fantasy be conducted in a dimly lit room with a carpeted floor, so the participants can lie down comfortably. I allow the participants a few minutes to settle down before asking them to close their eyes and to listen without asking questions. I then begin the script very slowly, in a nonabrasive voice. The script allows for maximum use of the individual participant's projection of her own personal experience since it is not very detailed. After each image, there is a long pause to allow the participants time to "picture" the situation. After I have finished talking, I allow the participants a few minutes to recover before we gather in a group again to discuss the experience.

In a parent group, I have used the following fantasy to increase the sensitivity of the parents to their child's world.

> You are your child. . . . Imagine waking up in your crib. . . . You look around your room. . . . Note how large everything seems. You have no hearing aids on. Imagine how quiet everything is. . . . Your mother comes in. Imagine looking up at her. . . . You are taken out of your crib and dressed. Your hearing aid is put in. Imagine how that must sound. . . . You are in your high chair having breakfast. Look around the room. . . . You are now being dressed to go out. . . . You are in your car seat. . . . You are brought into school. Imagine what the teachers and the other adults must look like. . . . You are taken to have your hearing tested. Imagine what the sounds sound like. . . . You return home in the car. Imagine that you are looking out the window. . . . You eat lunch. . . . You are put back into your crib. . . . You awaken and see your parents come into the room. . . . You play in the living room and the kitchen where your mother is. . . . You watch television. . . . You have dinner. . . . Your pajamas are put on. . . . Your hearing aids are taken off. . . . You are put back into your crib. The lights are out and you lie in bed.

I have used the following fantasy with professional groups, and sometimes with parent groups. It generally evokes very strong emotions from both parents and audiologists.

> You wake up and lie in bed for a moment. . . .
>
> Today is the day you are going to have your child's hearing tested.
>
> You get up and get dressed. . . .

You go down to your child's room and see him asleep in his crib. What do you feel? . . .

Your child wakes up; you dress him. . . .

Your child is in a high chair in the kitchen, eating breakfast. . . .

You put his coat on and bring him into your car to drive him to the hospital. . . .

You are going up the stairs. . . .

You get to the audiologist's office. . . .

You are sitting in the sound-proof room and loud sounds are all around you; your child does not respond to any of them. . . .

You are back in the audiologist's office and are being told your child is deaf. How do you feel? . . .

You are driving home from the hospital; your child is in his car seat.

You get home and take off your child's coat. . . .

You lie down on your bed. How do you feel?

Running

Recently I have been taking parent groups out running. I am somewhat hesitant to write about that because I have just begun the pursuit. The parents and I are enthusiastic about our activity; we run on the nondiscussion morning, and anyone within the program (including staff and students) can participate on an entirely voluntary basis. The running session lasts about one-half hour; not all parents go on a regular basis and several have opted not to continue. Those who have persisted (staff as well as parents) report many positive changes, aside from the very obvious physical benefits. They report a general feeling of well-being and an increased ability to cope better with life stresses. The running affords them a time-out experience during which they engage in an activity solely for themselves, free of any demands; it is a means for them to increase their self-esteem. Most of the participants had previously viewed themselves as unathletic and somehow deficient because of their unwillingness to compete. In fact, most of the parents had hated athletics and several had negative experiences to report.

Running is an excellent choice of physical activity because the ability to run requires no trained skills. Parents already have the knowledge necessary to run. The basic requisite is persistence; if they continue, they become reinforced by seeing the steady increase in the distance they can run. Running is also attractive as a choice of activity because it is so accessible. There is no need for elaborate equipment or a court or playing field. The Emerson group ran on a road behind the clinic and all the parents needed to provide were their running shoes. Other groups may find alternative activities, such as bicycling or swimming, which work as well for them as running does for us. The most important ingredient in an exercise program seems to be a slow, sustained, noncompetitive physical activity.

The group run provides an important social vehicle as well. It has afforded me a chance to chat with the parents even more freely than we could in group discussions, altering even further the traditional relationship between the parent and the professional. It is very hard to be "distant" when we are both sweating after a joint, strenuous physical effort. There is also the nonverbal aspect of the activity and a feeling of community that develops as the group runs together.

In addition, many very subtle mental changes occur. The runners seem to be (and report being) better centered psychologically and more in control of themselves and the events in their lives. The relationship between the physical aspects of running and its mental-emotional components needs to be investigated in much greater detail. Running seems to have considerable merit in the counseling process, and we plan to continue exploring its use with future parent groups.

Summary

Structured experiences are one way to influence group attitudes rapidly. The structured experiences of role playing, hypothetical families, and guided fantasies have been suggested as potentially useful techniques for facilitating a group. It must be stressed that those techniques are only supplemental in nature and must be part of a whole workshop experience, with maximum opportunity provided to process the experience. No structured experience can possibly replace a sensitive group leader.

Reference

1. Luterman, D.   "Hypothetical Families," *Volta Review* 71: 347, 1969.

6

The Impact of Deafness
on the Family

The family is a delicately poised system designed to meet the needs of its individual members. The "intrusion" of the handicapped child often disrupts that delicate balance and, therefore, families frequently need help to restore a healthy dynamic in which all members can nurture their personal growth. The sensitive professional will program for the entire family; he will help the parents, grandparents, siblings, and any other family members who are in close proximity, to adjust to the changed family's needs. The family can be viewed and treated as a unit: any time there is a disruption—such as the birth of a handicapped child—energy must be expended to maintain a precarious "family homeostasis," the delicate (family) balance in established relationships. The restoration of that balance often becomes the function of a family therapist [4], who deals with the family as a unit. This chapter is designed to explore ways in which relationships are changed in the family by the presence of a handicapped child.

Husband-Wife Relationship

By nature of the way in which our present society is structured, the bulk of "parent education" is really "mother education." Since most parent-directed, deaf-education programs meet during the day, the mother is (in the traditional family, at least) the only parent who can attend regularly. For the traditional family that has fairly strong sex-role identities, the parent-education program can and does place an enormous amount of strain on the husband-wife relationship. Many mothers begin to feel acutely the responsibility for child management and for weighty educational decision-making without benefit of a particularly informed or involved husband. Since the mother is receiving the education and the relevant information, the father often finds himself in a passive role, abdicating the full responsibility for those decisions to his wife. Many men in a traditional family setting, in which the man is expected to make all the important decisions, find that role-reversal very difficult to accept. The wives, on the other hand, often have difficulty in accepting their assertive role and, by extension, in viewing their husbands as being less competent than themselves. That ineffectuality is most obvious when the husband does therapy with the child at home; he is very often incapable simply because he has such limited experience and knowledge in child management. It may be difficult, however, for the husband (and sometimes for his wife) to accept direction from his wife, since it often seems like criticism. That situation can lead to arguments and defensiveness on the part of both husband and wife, and obviously it requires a restructuring of their relationship (which can be very painful).

The mixed-parent group, in which unrelated husbands and wives meet together, is very helpful toward overcoming the parents' defensiveness. The men seem to listen more to a woman other than their wives as she talks about the problems of relating with her husband; they can listen without having to take responsibility for any of the recounted behavior and they can listen objectively while still relating material to their own experiences. The women also respond nondefensively to the man's complaints. After several mixed-parent sessions, it is necessary to have a complete husband-and-wife group meeting to process what has transpired in the mixed sessions.

An alternative approach is the "fish bowl" technique, in which the mothers of the group sit in the center and the fathers watch from the periphery. The mothers discuss problems of husband-wife relationships while the men listen. After a period of time, the groups reverse and the fathers come into the center while the mothers observe from the outside. At the end of the session, we have a full-group discussion with husband-wife interaction. That technique seems to promote much freer discussion than does a total group discussion with eye-to-eye contact. The group in the center appears to forget rapidly about their spouses on the periphery, and the discussion is conducted among the members. When the total group meets, members can discuss individual points. The "fish bowl" helps to open up groups and only needs to be used once or twice before the group can proceed to a full-group discussion.

Despite our best efforts, the gap between the spouses (initially, at least) seems to widen. During their morning group sessions, the mothers frequently complain that they do not get enough emotional support from their husbands and, as a result, they are the sole family members who are confronting the emotional issues. The women seem, however, to be more comfortable in dealing with the emotional issues than do the men. In our culture at present, most men do not seem to be comfortable in dealing with emotions; they prefer to deal with tangible issues and with facts that can be manipulated. Fathers, when they do get involved, tend to take a much longer-range view and become concerned about vocational issues, political issues, and fiscal problems of supporting a deaf child. The women, on the other hand, tend to stay with the daily management issues and are much more willing to deal with emotional issues.*

It would be a mistake to respond to the mothers' pleas of trying to get more emotional support from their husbands by pushing hard for affect in the fathers' groups or by telling (exhorting) them to provide their wives with emotional support. That approach will not work, particularly the exhortation, which is a violation of the nondirective facilitative norm to accept a group as it is at a particular time. It also may not be in the best long-term interests of those families to encourage the men to display large amounts of feeling to the exclusion of carrying out their traditional family role.

---

* Those generalizations do not, of course, hold for specific families. We have had families in which the roles have been reversed—both emotionally and structurally—whereby the father has not been the principal source of family income and has been the participating family member, while his wife has related to the Emerson program in a more peripheral way. Families have been changing, allowing more freedom for both husband and wife; nevertheless, the overwhelming predominance of my clinical experience has been with the traditional family, structured along fairly standard sex-role stereotypes.

There may be a need in the family for both approaches—
the more intuitive *now* affect approach that most women
seem to give, and the more intellectual, factual, long-range
planning that most men seem to bring to the relationship.
Those functions are complementary and, if properly har-
nessed, they can work in the best interests of the child. In
those relationships that do not allow for much change, the
parents must learn to accept each other for what each can
give and to seek elsewhere that which is still lacking. Women
who cannot find emotional support within their marriages
may need to find it elsewhere, for example, in the parent-
support groups run by schools or in parent organizations.

The expressed need for emotional support may expose
many other deficiencies in the husband-wife relationships, and
many marriages complicated by special-needs children have
ended in divorce. In the families we have observed, the parents' divorce seemed to be precipitated by the added stress of
the hearing-impaired child on an already weak relationship.
Sometimes divorce has occurred as a result of the parents'
personal growth, a recognition of their own strength and
autonomy, and a preference to do so. We have also seen (and
parents have reported) the opposite outcome; that is, marriages have been strengthened by the experience of having a
deaf child, whose presence becomes a rallying point for the
parents as well as for the rest of the family. For the parents,
the handicapped child can offer an opportunity to restructure
a relationship that has perhaps become stale. Men have often
reported how delighted they were to find out how much
strength their wives showed, and the women have expressed

delight at the caring qualities that emerged from their husbands. Often, both parties find a new purpose in working very hard together in parent organizations and therapy programs, and by so doing, strengthen the bond between them. Families in which good communication between the husband and wife is well established (or can be established through a parent program) seem to survive and grow; families in which there is poor communication seem to be destroyed.

Parents-Grandparents Relationship

In addition to the role-reversal that frequently occurs between the husband and wife, another reversal occurs between the parents of the deaf child and their own parents. The grandparents frequently become fixated in the denial stage; it is difficult for them to deal with both the pain of having a handicapped grandchild and with the knowledge that their own child is suffering. That experience creates a formidable, emotional situation for them to deal with, and it comes at a time in life when they are perhaps least prepared to cope with emotional emergencies. The grandparents, like most nonprofessionals, lack information and knowledge about deafness. Consequently, their children (the parents of the hearing-impaired child) frequently know far more than they do, and they are also much further advanced emotionally. The parents, through professional contacts and parent education groups, rapidly acquire information and perhaps emotional support to help them move through the mourning stages faster than the grandparents can. Furthermore, if the mother and father seek support from their parents, frequently it is not available; rather, that in-between generation often has to "parent" its own parents by providing them with information and emotional support. The young parents often deeply resent that role-reversal because they want so badly to be mothered and fathered and have no such comfort available.

There is a famous Mark Twain quip to the effect that, "When I was 16, I thought my father was the stupidest man alive; when I was 20, I was surprised to see how much he had learned in four short years." Although that saying may be true of the adolescent experience, it is not true of the adult experience. For all of us, there comes a time when we realize that we truly do know more about our own lives than our parents do; we must experience the exquisite loneliness of being adult and of being fully responsible for ourselves. That realization is always a very painful process and people experiencing it go through a crisis reaction. Having the deaf child accelerates the process so that a time of renewed stress in the parent-grandparent relationship occurs. Many parents complain that their parents are a real burden to them rather than a support, that is, the grandparents push them to go to another doctor or to seek some cure—such as acupuncture—when the parents are well past that denial point in their development. Very often, the grandparents respond with anger and become very hostile. As one daughter-in-law put it,

She had begun to love and trust her daughter-in-law, and then I'd betrayed the trust. I was supposed to present their son with a fine, healthy, and above all, "normal" child. That wasn't a lot to expect. Anyone could do it.

Instead, I had given birth to a "defective baby." In so doing, I had threatened her son's well-being—or her image of it. I had threatened his financial future, his emotional make-up, his position in the community, and his mobility and independence. Her harsh words to me in the hospital were a way of expressing the same protectiveness toward her son that I was now feeling toward mine [2].

Grandparent groups can be very helpful and occasionally parents have requested us to hold parent-grandparent discussion groups. The "fish bowl" technique seems to be very effective in such cases. We have also urged parents to bring their own parents to observe the nursery, so that I might have a chance to meet and talk with them informally. This is one of the few places where reassurance from the professional is needed; reassuring the grandparents gives the parents some breathing room, and it gives the grandparents another source of information and support.

Not all the relationships between parents and grandparents are negative. Occasionally, the grandparents have been more capable than the parents and have assumed primary care of the child. In those cases, they respond much like parents, the only difference being that they are somewhat older and wiser; they are generally quite delightful to work with.

Parents frequently discover that the child's grandparents are an important resource for them, although not in the way they had originally expected. Grandparents frequently provide respite care, via very necessary baby-sitting, so the parents can have some time out. Grandparents can also provide very necessary parenting to the other siblings in the family when the parents are overwhelmed by the demands of the handicapped child. The surrogate-parent role played by the grandparents can become very important for the emotional well-being of the normal siblings. The restructured relationship between the parents and grandparents can also be a very exciting one; for the first time, the parents can begin to feel and respond as adults when dealing with their own parents and, in turn, find themselves being treated as adults.

Siblings

If not handled properly by the parents, the handicapped child can present enormous emotional problems for the normal sibling. Very often, the sibling gets proportionately less of his parent's time and energy because so much is being taken up by the handicapped child. It is not uncommon for siblings to develop a pseudosensory deficit in an effort to gain some parental attention. Although that occurrence is a rather extreme attention-seeking device, other more common strategies have included school failures, illnesses, and frequent tantrums. Those tactics are assertive measures that are usually taken to arouse parental concern and to achieve the goal of getting attention. The gravest—and most insidious—problem, however, may be the very "good," uncomplaining child who carries some deep-seated, unexpressed resentments. That child can and does grow up without having some of his very fundamental needs met.

Siblings are frequently asked to assume many responsibilities at a much earlier age than they would be ordinarily, if there were not a handicapped child in the family. For example, they are often called on to baby-sit while the harried parents are rushing off to another parents' meeting or doctor's appointment. Also, the sibling may feel and respond to the parents' embarrassment and may not want to be seen with, or to take care of, the handicapped child in public. (An exception is the one family that apparently did such a beautiful job with the whole family's attitude that the deaf child was brought into the first-grade class for "Show and Tell"!) The issue of embarrassment seems to be most acute for adolescent siblings. At a time when they want most to blend in with their peers, they may become identified as "the brother of the deaf kid," which may be very painful for them.

The solutions to the sibling problem are easy to grasp intellectually but are very often difficult to achieve practically. The parents need to direct attention to the sibling as a person—not just as a vehicle to help them produce a well-functioning handicapped child. The sibling needs to be incorporated into all family discussions regarding his own welfare; he also needs attention in his own right. That balance is not always easy for the parents to accomplish because they are expending so much energy on the handicapped child, on their own relationship, and on their relationship with their own parents. The various antagonistic forces within the family cause a formidable situation for the parents to deal with.

The topic of siblings occurs frequently in the parent group; parents are usually very aware of and concerned about inequities in the time and attention devoted to their respective children. Having sibling day in the nursery has been helpful in involving the normal-hearing children with their deaf siblings. (See page 66.) Parents also have found it helpful to set aside special time for the siblings and to have baby-sitters care for the handicapped child while they spend the day with their normal-hearing children. Grandparents can also frequently fill in as surrogate parents for the normal-hearing siblings.

Problems also arise in terms of unborn siblings. Parents are frequently faced with the painful decision of whether or not to have another child—especially when the deaf child is the first born. That issue is frequently discussed in parent groups; the decision about whether to have another baby (fathers are usually willing, mothers are more reluctant) seems to hinge, in part, on how well the deaf child is doing in relation to his parents' expectations. Parents who are feeling good about themselves and their child's progress generally tend to opt for having another baby; those who are encountering more difficulties tend to defer pregnancy. The issue is very complex and involves many variables related to family expectations and economics. Unfortunately, conventional genetic counseling is generally so vague that it is rather useless in helping parents to reach a decision. A fairly large number of parents who have been through the Emerson program have chosen to increase their families; some have had a second deaf child.

The counselor must take no responsibility for the parents' decision; it is often an agonizing one and parents need the time and the space provided by the group to discuss that issue. Generally, the issue seems to center less on whether or not the newborn would be a deaf child (although that is a major concern) than on the continued restriction of the mother in

the traditional role as a housewife. I think that outlook reflects women's increasing awareness of their alternatives to
mothering and also the general change in expectations regarding the woman's role in the family. There no longer seem
to be any simple answers, and each family has to struggle
toward its own solution. Because of the increasing amount of
stress that families must learn to accommodate, families are
changing. Furthermore, most of those changes are very positive, allowing for all members to grow and for a more democratic family structure to emerge.

Parents as People

All too often, in a parent program there is a failure to recognize the parents' own needs for personal growth and for
some time out from dealing with deafness. Parents can become very unidimensional—that is, think solely in terms of
their child's deafness. For some, that can lead to a great deal
of resentment, or to the "martyred mother" syndrome. That
syndrome seems to afflict mothers more than fathers, although
occasionally we have seen a martyred father. The parent frequently becomes a martyr as a result of parental guilt feelings
—it is seen partly as a kind of retribution for having in some
way caused the deafness and partly from a perception of parenthood as a noble, self-sacrificing role in which the parents'
personal needs are always met last. The martyred parent is
very resentful and often says to the child, in deed (if not in
words), "Look at all I have done for you!" The child may
then begin to feel vaguely guilty himself; he may feel that he

is never really satisfying the unhappy parent and may never feel worthy of receiving time and material things that are given in such a grudging manner. The child of a martyred parent is usually guilt-ridden and has a very low self-esteem.

Sometimes the best therapy for the child is a vacation for the parents. Also, we have found the parents' day off to be a very useful technique. It sends a clear message to the parents that we, the staff, feel it is important that they take time for themselves and that there are other people who can do the necessary job with their child. When successful, that technique can lead to a more relaxed, receptive parent who works much more effectively with her child.

The Parent of the Adolescent

Very little is written about the adolescent handicapped child, let alone his parent, on whom there is no information at all. Correspondingly, programs for the parent of the adolescent are severely lacking. On the preschool level, many programs are aimed (at least ostensibly) toward the parent. As the child reaches school age, however, and certain educational decisions have been made (in particular, regarding schooling and methodology), both the parent and the child seem to become latent, and parental contact and involvement in the child's schooling is minimal. However, when her child reaches adolescence, the parent frequently has another crisis. She becomes aware that she has been "sleeping" and that the schools have not been effective in training her child with good communicative and/or vocational skills; the child of 16 or 17 years of age is still not able to communicate. The parent must realize once again the responsibilities of parenting, and a crisis reaction similar to that experienced at the time of the diagnosis of deafness takes place. That later crisis, though, is more emotionally difficult because the parent really experiences "failure" in a very deep sense—failure that can no longer be leavened by any fantasy (as it often was in the preschool years) that her child would be a very "successful" deaf person. The feelings of shock, anger, depression, guilt, and so on all emerge once again. At that point, the parent needs very badly the support and help of a sensitive professional and, perhaps, a parent-support group.

For most parents, the fundamental issue of parenting is one of "letting go"; that is, allowing the child responsibility that he can handle successfully. On the one hand, if the parent uses no controls at all, the child may experience many failures, which will reduce his self-esteem; on the other hand, if the parent does not let the child take any responsibility, she sends the child a message that he is incapable of doing very much, which also reduces the child's self-esteem. The sensitive parent needs to operate somewhere between those two extremes—within an area that is often very small.

Parents of special-needs children frequently underestimate their child's ability and do not allow him enough freedom to make mistakes. A frequent concomitant of parents' guilt feelings is an overprotective stance; parents who did not work through their guilt feelings during the child's preschool years have a great deal of difficulty letting go when he becomes an adolescent. Ironically, parent-education programs can contribute to that problem by involving the parent with the child so heavily that letting go at any level becomes difficult. It is very painful for some parents to realize that once their child reaches adolescence they may need him more than he needs them. The parent who has not developed outside resources and has devoted herself completely to her child frequently panics at the thought that she will no longer have anyone on whom to focus her energies; that is, that her status as a parent of a handicapped child will change shortly, and she will have to find a new status. That step can be, and often is, very threatening for some parents, who need considerable help from professionals and from other parents to adjust.

Normal adolescence is a painful experience for both the parent and the child. The child is fulfilling his biological mandate to separate from the parents and to establish himself as a functioning adult. The parent needs to readjust constantly to the gradual changing reality of the child's impending adulthood. Consequently, considerable stress is imposed on the relationship that needs to be dealt with continually. As the child pushes against previously imposed limits, the parent must yield just enough to allow the child room to grow. The problem with the handicapped child is that he, if he has not been accorded any responsibility, will not push at those limits. In fact, he may not even be aware that limits exist. In that case, the parents may feel very comfortable because there seems to be so little stress; the result, however, will be an overly dependent adult. For the parent of the adolescent, it often seems as though there is no winning.

Following are some examples of responses to a question-naire about being the parent of a deaf adolescent.

1. *The major problem facing parents of a teenaged deaf child:*

"Seeing him struggle to blend in with his peer group (all of whom hear). He wants to be with his peer group."

"She doesn't understand why she has to be deaf, and I really don't have the answers for her, and it is hard for her to communicate with hearing people, and it frustrates her."

"Keeping everything running more or less smoothly. There is never any end to it. Both my wife and I work to keep all of our son's teachers informed and calm. At the same time, we have to do the same thing with our son and his sisters."

"Decision-making!! I am really tired—physically and men-tally—from making decisions and following up what needs to be done. There are times I'd like to be free of it all but I know that I never will be."

"The amount of dependency required of me because of the lack of companionship of her peers due to deafness."

2. *The uniqueness of parenting a deaf child:*

"Lack of alternatives and limitations of possibilities."

"The extra time required to assist with language acquisition and homework assignments (clarification and under-standing)."

"I expect I'll have a lot more trouble 'letting go' and let-ting her be independent."

"It seems to me that we have to deal with more details than we do for the hearing children and every situation involves feelings which are more intense than normal. Many of the problems our son has are not very different from those of hearing children. . . ."

"We lack the necessary subtlety of vital communication available to parents of normal-hearing teenagers." (Many of the parents felt that their problems were not very dif-ferent from parents of normal-hearing children.)

3. *The major problem as the deaf child sees it (as reported by the parents):*

"She is behind most children her age at school."

"She misses being with more deaf friends. She has trouble talking on the telephone."

"Lack of acceptance by others."

"Making close friends and keeping them."

"Peer acceptance."

"An embarrassment that sometimes he is not understood by people; a desire for independence and still being de-pendent on others in dealing with the outside world."

"Wanting to feel part of things and often missing out because of hearing loss, resulting in frustration."

(Almost all parents saw the problem as being social in nature.)

4. *Dealings with professionals:*

"At this time, positive. Even though we had few professionals acquainted with hearing loss and its implications in our school system, most seem eager to learn and implement suggestions—teachers particularly."

"As a whole, I guess I feel professionals give answers rather than information and deny parents the opportunity to learn and grow."

"Medical professionals, in the beginning, seemed unable to face *my* fears and to treat them as if they were real."

"Most medical professionals are not aware enough of deafness or what it means to a family. . . . Some professionals treat parents as if they know nothing about their own children. Some type of course in teacher-parent relationships should be required."

"My contact with professionals has been mediocre at best. I entertain the idea that our son is ours. What we want for him is a combination of his interests and desires and our own. The tone of most of the meetings concerning our son has been more along the lines of 'Here is what you want.' Each of the professionals comes to our case with his own background, interests, and prejudices. I would like to see them try to understand what our family's values and expectations are before they begin offering suggestions. I would also like to see people admit when they don't know what they are doing. Professionalism sometimes gets in the way of this."

The last parent has said it so well and, unfortunately, reflects a sizable segment of the parent reaction. The one other question asked of the parents was regarding the kind of program they felt was needed. Almost all of them articulated a desire for some parent-support group in one way or another. The sample is biased in that most of the responders are graduates of the Emerson program and have had some positive experience in a support group. (Recently, we offered a five-session group to parents of adolescent children and the reports of the parents in that group were highly positive—if for no other reason than that the group provided them with a chance to feel less alone in grappling with the rather awesome task of raising an adolescent child who happens to be handicapped.)

Professionals need to address themselves to the problems faced by the parent of the adolescent and to initiate programs for them. The programs for parents of adolescent children should be a continuation of existing school programs. The problem really begins after the preschool program, when schools generally reduce severely their parent programs (usually in deference to PTA meetings and teacher-parent conferences). During those latency years, many unhealthy attitudes can develop concerning child-management issues; parents need continuous help (although perhaps not as much as they did during the crisis-plagued preschool years) to receive some form of support and information. The program should be intensified during the adolescent years, when problems seem to become more acute. Schools should also consider working with mixed parent-adolescent groups; such techniques as "fish bowling" and mixed grouping could also be employed. Rossett [3] has developed and described a technique in which groups of parents and their deaf adolescents view transparencies that show various family situations; questions are then posed by the group leader to the audience to stimulate discussion. That rather innovative use of media has not yet been evaluated sufficiently.

Obviously, a corpus of research must be established regarding what happens between the parent and the handicapped child when he reaches adolescence. At present, there is a glaring lack of data in the field that prevents us from fully identifying the problems and determining the effectiveness of therapeutic programs.

If one dwells on all the problems of raising handicapped children as well as on the problems of developing programs, one may possibly become depressed. I agree with Moores' observation:

> It is wrong to paint a completely depressing picture of the situation. Despite the fact that deaf individuals usually receive inadequate instruction in language, speech, and school subjects; that their parents are miscounseled and misled; that they face prejudice, distrust and discrimination—in spite of all of this, the majority of deaf people make an adequate adjustment to the world. They marry, raise children, pay taxes, contribute to

the good of the community, fight, watch television, and entertain themselves in much the same way as everyone else. Most of their problems are caused by the dominant society. Deaf people have survived and endured in the face of an indifferent world that must be dealt with daily [1: p. 102].

Summary

The handicapped child presents many problems to the family structure: the relationship between parents and their parents, sibling interactions, and the marital dynamics are all placed under stress. Programs need to accommodate the changing family dynamics—particularly for the parent of the adolescent, who is at crisis again, a situation that is seldom recognized by the professional. Support groups for parents of adolescent children are vitally needed and should be an outgrowth of the programs available to elementary-school students.

References

1. Moores, D. *Educating the Deaf: Psychology, Principles, and Practices.* Boston: Houghton Mifflin, 1978.
2. Pieper, E. "Grandparents Can Help." *The Exceptional Parent* 6:7-11, April, 1976.
3. Rossett, A. "Special Strategies for a Special Problem: Improving Communication Between Hearing Impaired Adolescents and Their Parents." *Volta Review* 76:231-238, April, 1974.
4. Satir, V. *Conjoint Family Therapy.* Palo Alto: Science and Behavior Books, 1967.

7

The Educator and the Parent

Historically, the relationship between the parent and the educator has been an intimate one. Schools resulted from a group of parents convening and deciding that the children of the community needed to be educated. Then they sought out and hired the teacher, who frequently lived with families in the community. There was a direct and rather simple relationship between the consumers (parents) and the producer (teacher), with the parents being very much involved in all aspects of the educational process. Only relatively recently (where communities have become large enough to have centralized schools) have layers of bureaucracy intervened between the parent and educator. Elected school boards and superintendents of schools were created to cope with the larger-scale system. Now, principals, counselors, and an entire state bureaucracy all interfere with direct teacher-parent communication. In fact, most school communication seems to take place among the bureaucrats. Unfortunately, most parents have forgotten about the origins of schools and frequently operate as though the schools belonged to the bureaucrats. To correct that situation, the parents must, and have begun to, assert their rights. The recent emphasis on consumerism parallels the efforts of parents to obtain more direct control of the educational process.

The Parent and P.L. 94-142

At the present time, there is a very strong effort on the part of both legislators and parents to establish parents' rights. As a result, parents now have many more legal options open to them than have been available in the past regarding their child's education. The most far-reaching effect of such legislation has been the passage of P.L. 94-142, the Education for All Handicapped Children Act. That law, passed in 1975, requires each school system to prepare an Individualized Education Program (IEP) for every handicapped child, and to attempt to educate all handicapped children in the least restrictive environment. The plan must be written by educators in conjunction with the parents. That specific aspect of the law should have a revolutionary impact on the current relationships between parents and educators. Educators can no longer view the parents as rather faceless appendages of their child; instead, they must view parents as concerned people with whom the schools must negotiate regarding educational planning and placement. Also, more face-to-face, parent-teacher contact will occur, because educators must permit the parents access to all the processes of planning for their child's education. Therefore, since both the educator and the parent want essentially the same thing for the child, if they can harness their energies and respective knowledge, the child will benefit enormously. The parent has a unique perspective and information about her own child, and the educator has access to the necessary educational material. By combining those essential factors, they can plan well together.

The implications of the Individualized Education Program are well stated by Testut and Baldwin [5: p. 285]:

> The IEP must be based on a comprehensive assessment, which requires increased communication and interaction of several professionals and the parents. Continuous reporting of progress involves maintaining the appropriateness of an IEP at periodic intervals. Flexibility of programming is required, so that a child can shift to different educational options. It is anticipated that a child will not remain in the same educational placement throughout his educational program but rather progress through increasing amounts of mainstreaming. Some children may need temporary periods in special classes or schools to meet changing developmental or psychosocial adjustments that occur during adolescence.

The parents cannot evade the responsibility for participating in their child's educational program and planning. At the very least, they will have to sign their approval to the educational plan. If they execute their rights fully, they will be in a position to check on their child's progress, monitor the school, and hold educators accountable for their programs.

The need for more informed parents will place increased responsibility on both the professionals who participate in parent-training programs and existing parent groups. The parent-training programs will have to produce the informed, nonintimidated, and interpersonally skillful parent who can participate fully with educators in the Individualized Education Programs. The parent groups will need to provide information to parents about their rights under the law, and, in some cases, provide parents who need help with a trained parent-advocate to assist them at IEP meetings.

The possible repercussions of P.L. 94-142 over the long term are very exciting. Everyone can benefit—educators will have to become more sensitive to parents; parents will have to take more responsibility; and the individualized planning, if done with care, will be of immense value to the child. Nevertheless, a large potential for developing an adversary relationship between the educator and the parent will still exist, particularly if both respond defensively. In the short term, as with any change, a great deal of stress, anger, and frustration will be expressed. All those concerned will need to learn new behaviors. I can only hope that that negative phase is truly short term and can be weathered by responsible professionals, without reverting to old strategies of dealing with parents, and that parents can maintain their contact and communication with the schools.

The issue of educational placement is very complex, involving more than the child's immediate educational needs. Placement entails issues concerning parental values, family needs related to living style, and the availability of programs within the community. For example, the problem encountered by Mr. and Mrs. H. in the section on hypothetical families was an actual situation. The issue there was whether or not the family should move to avoid placing their child in a residential school program. Moving involved uprooting the whole family, whereas not moving meant that the handicapped child would be separated from the rest of the family. At issue was the value of having the child live at home. After much discussion, the family decided to move closer to the school so the child could live at home, and both she and her father commuted. I have no way of knowing if that was the "right" decision for that family to make. The parents wanted me to make the decision for them, but I could not do that. The professional must not impose his value system on the parents—they are the ones who have access to all the data for making the necessary decisions, and they are the ones who must live with the results. The aim of the professional must be to give the parents the necessary confidence to make the decisions they must make. The only way confidence can develop is by the parents actually making their own decisions. The professional can and should provide information; but he must recognize that the wisdom for decision-making resides within the parent.

Educational planning must consider the individual personal needs of the child and the parents. Too often, plans are written solely in terms of the child's communication needs or the institution's needs without considering any of the family's needs. For example, the educational plan that requires the child to travel for over one hour to and from school may not be the best plan for the child in terms of his personal needs for free time, despite the fact that the school may be the best educational placement. The child's personal, emotional needs must be considered first, and I would hope that parents and other educators would place a very high priority on those. Educational deficits can be overcome relatively easily; personality maladjustments are much more difficult to work with and are very pervasive in all aspects of living. On the other hand, educational planning must allow the child to take risks. It is emotionally and educationally detrimental not to push at limits; without testing limits, the child's potential cannot be realized, and unused potential is probably the saddest loss in the field of deaf education. Fortunately, educational decisions are not irrevocable; mistakes can be corrected. Educators and parents must monitor their decisions and change course whenever indicated. Children can be hurt far more by not ever having had the chance to fail than by the occasional "failure" that is quickly rectified.

A father [1] of a deaf child, writing about his "disastrous" educational experience with his child, has commented in the following way:

Looking back, we learned a great deal from that initial disaster.

We learned that children are more resilient than parents. K. recovered from the experience a lot faster than my wife!

We learned the necessity of constant monitoring of the children's placements. Any initial reluctance to interfere was wiped out by that situation.

We learned that very often educational placement decisions are made more for their financial considerations than for the well-being of the child.

We learned the need for proper preparation of both the teacher and the other students when a deaf child is to be part of a class.

And most important of all, we learned that the child—not the professionals or the parents—is probably the best judge as to whether an educational situation is providing successful social living. Thus, we learned to rely on the children's signals.

Each educational year must be reviewed by educators and parents alike with an eye toward possible change. One of the most formidable educational problems has been the lock-step nature of the educational system. Children enter a school for the deaf and seldom leave until graduation. Rarely have they left because of the recognition of changing educational needs. A particular educational program must be viewed as a means to accomplish a particular end, and it should be altered if it is not meeting its goal. It is very clear that children and parents are unique; no single program can meet all families' needs. A very encouraging development in educational planning has been the development of the multifaceted school for the deaf, which provides a variety of programs and allows the educator and parents maximum flexibility in planning programs within the same facility [3]. We hope that more schools can move toward that concept.

Educational Placements

Various educational options are open to parents, including residential placement, day-class programs, and mainstreaming.

Residential Placement

In residential placement, the contract between the parent and the school clearly states that the school will assume the bulk of the responsibility for educating the child. In most cases, parent contact is minimal, usually limited to one or two individual teacher conferences a year, and perhaps including an occasional "public relations" type of meeting with all the parents.

Residential placement is a viable option that may be chosen by sensitive, caring, and competent parents after they have viewed all the educational alternatives; for example, the parents who see that their particular family structure cannot bear the stress of their particular deaf child living at home full time might opt for residential placement. Also, in some family situations, the parents cannot cope with their child; in those cases, the school can do a much better job than the parent by providing consistent educational management. One parent who selected a residential program wrote the following:*

Dear David,

Even though it's been four years since J. came home from S. [school for the deaf], many of my feelings during that period are still fresh in my mind. I'll share some with you.

J. was a bright and engaging young child. She had excellent preschool training, a supportive home, and was "doing well" by the standards of the time. More importantly, although we didn't fully realize it, T. and I were beginning to "do well" also. We had had the benefits of intensive parent education and were on our way to making educational decisions with confidence.

Prior to S., J. spent two years in a new day-class program within the public schools. We were house-hunting at the time and a reasonable commute for her was an important consideration in our choice of community. I visited her classroom often and it soon became apparent to me she was not realizing her potential. I had a mixture of feelings—anger, disappointment, and fright. Maybe she would never speak or write in sentences.

---

* This letter and subsequent ones in this chapter were solicited by me from parents who had been in the Emerson program and are now or have had experience with the particular educational program being discussed.

. . . Maybe, maybe. . . . I had many of the same thoughts I had experienced when we first found out she was deaf—mainly a dread of the future.

We began thinking seriously about S. J. was now six. We were also feeling pressures from outside our family. T. was among a group of parents who had worked hard to start day-class programs after the rubella epidemic and we were criticized for leaving one. J.'s teacher felt she was doing well and there was no need for change. But we knew the time had come.

J. entered S. in September, 1970. We felt devastated. It was easier for me to accept than T.—I think because I had spent so much time observing her in the day class. We both wanted a program with a solid curriculum and, at that period, only the schools for the deaf seemed to have one.

I remember the first weekend we picked her up. She started to cry the moment she saw us and we joined her. All she complained about was the peas and carrots, but I'm sure there was more on her mind than that. Time passed and we became adjusted to the weekend horrors—a four-hour round-trip drive on Friday, and an exhausted, grumpy child who walked in the door and checked immediately what possessions of hers had been touched. Academically, we were thrilled. She was learning. The school kept us as well informed as possible under very difficult circumstances. We were encouraged to visit, but how often can you stop in 94 miles away? The days were long and we were worried that she was losing identity with her family. She had joined another family and we had entrusted them with the most important aspects of her growth. What kinds of values was she developing? What about her religious training? What about her feelings toward her sister and brother? Actually, for us, the break from a deaf-centered home was a relief—something we had never anticipated. We relaxed and enjoyed our other children.

During the latter part of J.'s third year at S. it became obvious that she would be ready to leave soon. The school had advanced her several times and we began looking for alternative programs. Now we were more confident in our decisions. We found a small independent girls' school where J. felt comfortable. She was now almost 11 and helped us choose her new school. She left S. very sadly. She still corresponds with her friends faithfully and spends a few days there every year.

This year J. is in eighth grade and receives academic tutoring in ancient history and English. She is doing amazingly well and has rejoined the family mentally and emotionally. In retrospect, we are very grateful we had the confidence to make the decision to send her to S. Parents of handicapped children make many trade-offs which are difficult to weigh. There is no perfect solution.

J. feels she has the same academic choices open to her as any other bright, hardworking student. We feel this is in large measure due to the solid language base she received at S.

That family has demonstrated the willingness to change when a program was no longer meeting their needs. I cannot help but admire the courage of those parents for making their painful decisions.

Residential placements are much harder than other alternatives for parents to select; making that choice leads to even more feelings of guilt and condemnation by relatives and, sometimes, well-meaning but insensitive friends. I have learned to trust the parents' judgments and I do not question parents who elect to send their child to a residential school. I recognize now how painful that decision is to make and how much courage is often needed to sustain it.

Residential schools can, theoretically, do more for parents than they commonly do in practice. They could provide parent-support groups (perhaps on a short-term basis, such as a weekend) to discuss the feelings about placing a child in a residential program. They also could provide a "hot-line" program, whereby parents of older children would be available to parents of newly enrolled children. Specifically, a short-term, intensive, parent-residential program might provide the parents with needed information and skills to relate more fully to the educators and to their child. In particular, the parents seem to need help managing the weekends at home, and an ongoing counseling program emanating from the school would probably be of immense help to them. The school administrators and teachers need to be concerned about the home environment of the child on weekends and holidays; if possible, a home-visitation program would probably be desirable, especially if supplemented with increased teacher-parent contact.

The Day-Class Program

The day-class program is a compromise between the residential program and the mainstreamed program, which attempts to provide the best features of both and often fails to accomplish either. In the day-class category, I include the day class held within a public school as well as the autonomous day school for the deaf. Both of those programs have equal access to the child in the course of a school day, and both seem to have vague contracts with parents concerning areas of responsibility. It is moot whether or not the professional has enough access to the child so she can feel as comfortable in assuming responsibility for most of the child's education as professionals do in a residential program. Programs seem to vary in terms of how much parent participation they expect. A high degree of participation is generally expected of parents at the preschool level; as the children get older, the schools seem to involve the parents less and less. Many of the day programs provide for a Parent-Teacher Association (unfortunately, most activities are concerned with fund-raising), some evening information meetings, periodic meetings with the teacher, and, perhaps, some school visitation by the parents. Rarely is there any parent-support group. A parent of a child in a day class writes:

Dear David,

Our daughter K. was almost two years old before we discovered that she had been born with a profound hearing loss. Although we soon learned that there was no corrective medical treatment, we were able to "do something about it" educationally almost immediately. We enrolled as a family in a parent-centered program for preschool deaf children. Thus, by the time she was three, we knew that there was a wide variety of educational settings available for her and that we, as her parents, must be the ones to ultimately decide which one would be best for her—at least for the coming year. We had also learned that we must take one year at a time. We visited a large variety of schools and programs before we decided to send her to a day class for the hearing impaired in a public school in a neighboring town. We have been fortunate that through the years this has continued to be a good placement for her, but we have reached that decision only after agonizing debate and discussion each spring with other parents, teachers, and administrators, all trying to ensure not only that this was indeed the best program for her needs, but also that the program would continue to exist from one year to the next. The lack of long-range planning in public deaf education continues to be our greatest frustration, despite supportive state and (now) federal legislation.

Many factors went into our original choice of a day class and continue to affect our decisions. We liked the program's philosophy that "this is a child who is deaf" (not "the deaf child" stereotype). We appreciated the open, friendly atmosphere and the way our child was welcomed into the activities of the class when we visited. We were pleased by the receptive attitude toward parent involvement. An adaptability and willingness to change as the needs of the child dictated was also an important aspect.

We felt that parent-professional cooperation was vital to help us to understand what and how our child was learning and how we could help the process. This day-class program offered just such cooperation. We have always been welcome in the classroom. Mothers of preschool children spend a morning a week in the classroom observing, helping, and teaching. Of course, having K. in a program comparatively close to home made this possible.

Having the school fairly accessible has also meant that we could talk to other parents of children in the program, sharing problems—and joys—perhaps unique to our "low incidence" world. Our parents' group, which meets monthly, has been important to all of us for both information sharing and socializing.

Being able to have K. living at home, experiencing in many ways the same kind of school day as her peers, has, of course, been a joy to us. We have stayed a close family, able to enjoy a great deal of time together (even working on that never-ending homework!). It is important to us that K. stay an integral part of the family, and that includes having her other relatives— grandparents, aunts, uncles—see her often and know her as a real child. It also means that she can play with the children in the neighborhood. Unfortunately, there are not many children in the immediate neighborhood and not a great deal of opportunity to meet others. Her classmates at school come from a wide geographical area, and inviting a friend over to play after school can become a real chore of planning and chauffeuring. The transportation situation also makes it impossible to participate in after-school activities unless the parent can do the driving. Transportation has remained a recurring problem over the years. We quickly learned that, although we had chosen a school in the next town, being the first one picked up and the last one brought home can turn a twenty-minute ride into an hour and a half. Transportation requires constant monitoring and quickly transforms the mild-mannered, fatalistic mother into a consumer activist!

Despite the transportation difficulties, the children in that small, special class have become close, hopefully lifelong, friends. Nonetheless, we wanted even more for our daughter, and the day class offered another benefit—the possibility of mainstreaming children into regular classrooms if and when they seem ready for this, and for as much or as little time as each child needs. The "regular" classes are, in a situation like this, readily available just down the hall. More importantly, the staff of the hearing-impaired program is there to lend support, provide some "in-service training," and monitor the child's progress. That simple walk down the hall to first-grade math turned out to be a minor disaster for our daughter. Nevertheless, we were glad to have had the chance to try it, glad to have had a knowledgeable and sympathetic staff to monitor her and consult with us when it became apparent that this was a poor placement. Several years later, partial mainstreaming at the fourth-grade level was an undeniable success. And in the interim years, K. had had the benefit of social integration at gym, art, lunch, etc. (She is now, at 11, fully mainstreamed in sixth grade, sharing a tutor with two other deaf children.) The willingness to adapt the program to our individual child's needs has been invaluable.

The experience of having a child with a low-incidence special need has made our lives busier and busier since we have gone on to become involved in local and statewide parents' groups and other regional and national organizations. Our concern for improved education soon expanded from concern over our child's world to that of all hearing-impaired children. An apparent void in professional leadership makes the participative parent's role in such organizations even more important.

Addenda: Our son, born three years after K., is also profoundly deaf. He, too, has been in the day class, but with a much different mixture of separate classroom time and mainstreaming, a different approach toward him as an individual child. We are pleased with this placement, also, but much soul-searching is done each year and we are never sure where either child will be in a year or two.

Despite the fact that those parents have remained in the same program, it is clear from their letter that they are very much involved in their child's educational plan and are constantly evaluating its suitability for their family. They demonstrate a clear willingness to risk, as shown by their placing their daughter in the math class, risking her lack of success academically. Furthermore, although these parents are clearly willing to take risks with their children, they also monitor the results carefully. Despite the child's "failure," she seems to be doing quite well.

The following letter is from a parent who opted for a day-school setting—that is, she sends her child to a school exclusively for the deaf, on a daily commuting basis. The first school she describes functions much in the traditional mode concerning relationships with parents; the second school has obviously tried some different approaches with parents.

Dear David,

For the last seven years, my son, S., has attended a day school for the deaf. The one big plus is having him home so he can enjoy the give and take of a large family. The drawback to day school is the commute, which presents two problems: the child's physical needs and the lack of hometown friends. At one point, S. was in his taxicab five hours a day, which was a drain on his stamina. Leaving the house at 6:30 in the morning and returning home at 5:00 made it impossible for him to participate in local activities, such as Cub Scouts, Little League, etc. Also, it made for a lack of local playmates. I realize this is not the case for those who live near their school. Also, S.'s deaf friends from school are spread over such a wide radius that, in order for him to see them outside of school, planning ahead and driving are a necessity.

As far as family involvement is concerned, our experience with S.'s first school was on the negative side, but it is very positive with the school he now attends. At S.'s first school, the doors were always locked. I couldn't figure out if it was to keep the deaf kids in or outsiders out. I felt that they did not want to involve the parents in the educational experience of their children; parents' meetings tended to be large, formal, and, for the most part, boring and uninformative. One thing that will always stick in my memory is S. coming home with notes pinned to his shirt. Granted, a child of 6, 7, or 8 might lose a note from school, but, for some reason, this really struck me as dehumanizing.

The school S. now attends is small, less structured, and more informal. Two very detailed reports (sometimes running as long as 10 to 12 pages) are discussed between the parents and the teacher each year. The school is always open to visits by parents or siblings. The parents, I feel, are very involved in the educational process; they are committed to fund-raising activities for the school, and they share with the staff both the achievements and problems of the school. Most teachers and parents are on a first-name basis and share an annual picnic and a Christmas party. The atmosphere thus created makes it very easy as a parent to feel free to call the school about any problems that you have.

It is easy for professionals to lose sight of the sensitivities of the parents. For example, although pinning notes to the parent on the child's shirt provided a sure way of getting the note home, it also served to put that parent "off." One can only wonder about a school's communication system when teachers must resort to that method of contacting parents. It is also clear that there was not good communication between the school and the parent, since she did not feel free to tell the teachers how she felt about their method of sending notes home.

That parent also had to make the painful decision to change methodology. She writes further:

Until S. was ten years old, his educational environment had been oral. After his third year at a deaf day school, he was placed in a transitional class. On the advice of one of his former teachers, I watched his educational progress very carefully that year, because she really felt S. was having difficulty in an oral situation. The frustrations of communication were always with us. That, plus the fact of the passage of 766 [the Massachusetts equivalent of 94-142]—no one seemed to know exactly what it would mean for handicapped children. The discovery that one of my other children had dyslexia after having completed six grades in a so-called good suburban school system. Maybe the experts didn't have all the answers; the growing of consumerism—with the impetus to look at things more closely and to question—were all factors that led me to seek another educational solution for S.

Still, I did not feel overly qualified to make this decision on my own, so S. went into the Hospital for Children for a week of testing. The conclusion reached was that S. was really falling behind in an oral setting and that a school with total communication would best suit his needs. In the meantime, we had visited the only deaf day school with total communication in the state and had been impressed by the quality and caliber of the staff, the good ratio of students to teachers, but mainly by the ingredient of fun that had been injected into the learning process, which made the children enjoy going to school and learning. The first year there for S. was hard because he had a lot of catching up to do. Most of my children and I have taken sign-language courses and, although we are far from experts, we can all communicate! And I feel that that's what it's all about.

It is clear that the first school failed to counsel that parent regarding the child's success with oralism. The parent had to do a great deal on her own and had to seek an independent evaluation of the child's progress. There again, the parent has demonstrated the willingness to risk and change educational solutions when her child's needs were not being met.

Some of the day programs have provided parent-support groups and information meetings through the Parent-Teacher Association. Innovative teachers have used workbooks, which they send back and forth to the homes via the children; in one program, a tape recording is sent home so the parents can literally "hear" what the teacher may be trying to accomplish in working with the child's speech. The parents can also "talk" to the teacher via the tapes. I know of very few professionals in day programs, however, who are pleased with the level of parent participation. Several formidable barriers to good communications exist, and parents and educators will have to work very hard to overcome them. To do that, each individual school must examine its expectations for parents and then listen carefully to parents as they articulate their needs. Taking those needs into consideration, the school should then plan flexible programs. The parents will have to commit themselves to participating in the programs and will have to assert their needs to the educators.

Mainstreaming

Mainstreaming is the placement of the deaf child in a regular classroom in a public school. Of all educational options, that one puts maximum stress on both the parent and child. There are different degrees of mainstreaming, which vary from total immersion in the hearing situation to limited contact during instruction in nonacademic subjects. With the advent of P.L. 94-142, more hearing-impaired children will be fully mainstreamed since the law stresses placement in the least restrictive environment. The parent of a mainstreamed child writes:

Dear David,

We've been very fortunate in our dealing with the staff in W.; they have been cooperative and caring, and also quite enthusiastic about S.'s placement. They always felt that S. would "make it," when, at times, I was not sure at all. Part of the reason for their understanding of deafness is, I believe, because the head of the speech department is married to a profoundly deaf man. She therefore has a great knowledge of deafness and is quite determined about mainstreaming deaf children. Beyond that, she adds a dimension of personal warmth that is unique and quite wonderful.

The difficulties that arise have occurred not with the specialists (speech therapists, tutors, etc.), but with the classroom teachers. Even after we spend much time explaining to the teacher what deafness is, how deaf S. is, what her abilities and limitations are, the teacher seems to forget and does something incredibly dumb, such as the time in fifth grade when the teacher gave S. an oral spelling test of single words. Things like that tend to diminish S.'s self-image, even though S. knows it's beyond her.

My own *general* opinion of the professionals within the school system is that they are competent but not extraordinary; they mean well but they just don't know enough. I feel that I have to think through every inch of S.'s educational plan myself to make sure all bases have been covered. This is a burden that parents of mainstreamed children must carry.

S. was mainstreamed because she seemed quite able to learn in this setting. The impact of this course of action on the family was never taken into consideration. It has proved to be quite a challenge.

There are tremendous stresses put on a mainstreamed child. The social pressure is enormous. Because of this and the process of development in any adolescent, these years in junior high school are difficult. S. takes out her frustrations at home. It would certainly be easier if she went to a residential school for the deaf.

For B. and me, this is a strengthening process, but not an easy one. S.'s sisters are just like any other siblings; sometimes they adore her and sometimes they can't stand her.

The stresses on the family are very real; however, we have a strong family unit and have been able to cope. I must also say S. has brought us great joy and pride. She is such an interesting, creative child and very lovable. I would miss not seeing her if she were away at school.

What I'm saying is, yes, it's difficult—but it's worth it. I think S. is in the right placement because that's where she wants to be. She is doing very well, so for now we're O.K.

To be successful, mainstreaming must be implemented with a great deal of care. The hearing-impaired child needs educational support via tutors, speech therapists, educational audiologists, and sensitive classroom teachers who must, in turn, have support from the administration. The classroom teacher needs the most support; unfortunately, in practice, she often receives the least. My experience with classroom teachers has generally been positive. They usually have very little information about deafness and, therefore, they are anxious and fearful when they see the deaf child come walking into the room "all wired for sound." So much of education is predicated on clear communication; when that avenue appears to be blocked, the teacher (understandably) becomes terrified. There must be clear support systems of tutors and teachers of the deaf built into the program to assist the teachers. Rather than limiting mainstreaming to an individual child, some schools have attempted to mainstream a whole class of hearing-impaired children, complete with their teacher. That form of mainstreaming eliminates the isolation problem for the hearing-impaired child and places a trained teacher of the deaf in the classroom to work with the regular teacher. That approach seems so appropriate that I wonder why it is not being used more frequently.

The parent must be very vigilant and informed about what is happening to her child in school; the contract in mainstreaming clearly calls for maximum parent participation. Mainstreaming has often meant isolation for the family because the parent does not have access to the parent group that is affiliated with a school for the deaf, and she has had to seek support and information from the statewide parent group instead. The professional must be keenly aware of the parents' need for affiliation; he may perhaps help to organize a "mainstreamed" parent group among parents in several public schools in the immediate region. That group could, in turn, provide social experiences for the children. Awareness of the social implications of mainstreaming are beginning to appear in the professional literature [4], and I suspect more attention will be paid to that subject in the future.

Counseling Parents Relative to Methodology

At some point—usually quite early in their experience with education of the deaf—the parents become aware of the controversy that exists in the field regarding the use of the sign system. That dispute has been in existence for over two hundred years, and it still does not seem amenable to a rational solution. Professionals seem to be very partial to one particular system, and they seek to "counsel" parents toward that approach.

Much of what passes for parent counseling is really parent manipulation; what the professional really seems to want to learn from counseling courses and texts are *techniques* he can employ to get the parent to do what the professional thinks the parent *should* do. Nowhere is that manipulative strategy more evident than in the area of methodology. "Counseling" in such a manner is the antithesis of the kind of counseling described and used in this book. The manipulative approach requires very selective listening on the part of the professional, who is always seeking ways to present his arguments in a winning manner. While the parent is talking, the professional is looking for the vulnerable spots, and is marshalling arguments, rather than responding to the parent's pain and confusion. The professional is in an adversary relationship, seeking to "win over" the parent. The "loser" parent then, is one with low self-esteem, who invariably ends up in a dependent relationship with the professional.

The saddest thing for me to see is a parent group riddled with the manual-oral controversy. The parents become more fanatical than the professionals because they have more at stake. The parents have taken a great risk by following a particular path which, they feel, has to be "the right one" for their child. Very often, the parents become the missionaries of a particular method, exhorting all others to follow them. That very rapidly rips apart parent groups, and it becomes very difficult to discuss any other issues in deaf education. Some states have had two parent groups, which has diminished the effectiveness of all the parents by sapping vitally needed energy from issues regarding the welfare of all deaf children. I have learned—in sometimes very painful ways—not to allow the methodology dispute to emerge when I am addressing some parent groups. Otherwise, I am seldom able to get beyond it.

It is the professional's responsibility to present, *when the parent is ready,* various educational alternatives in as factual and unbiased a manner as possible. I have found it best to have other professionals present their various points of view about deaf education, and then to help the parents sort out the presented data to come to some decision. The professional, too, needs to sort out his feelings about methodology and to prevent them from interfering with the parents' choices. At the very least, the professional needs to make his biases clear to the parents. The parents must be the ones to make the choice and to commit themselves to the particular approach. I do not think any approach can work unless there is a firm parental commitment; that is, if the child is enrolled in a program using some form of manual communication, then the parents must be willing to sign at home. Likewise, they must make a commitment to an oral approach if that is what the child is receiving in school.

The parents, however, must see the chosen approach as a vehicle geared toward education—as a means to an end, which, if not succeeding, must be discarded. They must accept the fact that other approaches may be quite satisfactory for other families and they must not become missionaries for any particular approach. The sanest stance on the methodology issue is articulated by Northern and Downs [2]:

Language is the desideratum that we most wish for the hearing-impaired. For too long we have been misled into placing oral speech as the primary goal for all these children, never realizing that the enrichment of their lives may be sacrificed for the ability to mouth words. What words? And in what relationships? If one is not able to think in highly complex language symbols, does it matter whether he is able to vocalize any of them? And, most important, how can he verbalize adequately unless he has an adequate symbol system to utilize?

The premise of our proposal for the management of the hearing-impaired child rests upon language as the primary goal to be sought for the child. Whatever route will lead the way through his neurologic labyrinth to reach language understanding, that route must be taken. We must be ruthless in discarding methods and methodologies, entrenched techniques nor any not yet established. Any, or all, should be selected . . . on the basis of what is best for the child, not for the institution. For too long the child has been forced to be tailor-made to the program; we must now tailor-make a program for each individual child's needs . . . [p. 264].

That should be the credo of all professionals working with parents of deaf children, because it enables the professional to put aside any doctrinaire considerations and to respond to the fears and confusions of the parents. It also empowers the professional to share his doubts and confusions with the parents so together they can embark on a search for the best educational vehicle for both child and parents.

In the section on role play, a situation between a teacher concerned about her "nonoral" pupil and the parent who wanted to have an "oral child" was described (see p. 119). It is possible to fantasize that situation:

TEACHER: I've called this meeting to give us a chance to get to know each other, and to discuss John. Are there some things you would like to know about me?

MOTHER: Yes. How is John doing?

TEACHER: Well, I am somewhat concerned because he seems to be having a difficult time in class. Have you noticed any difficulty at home?

MOTHER: He seems to come home very tired and very irritable.

TEACHER: It must be difficult for you.

MOTHER: It takes me a while to settle him down. I have to give him time to blow off steam.

TEACHER: What does he say about school?

MOTHER: He doesn't tell me very much. He just seems very tense.

TEACHER: How are you feeling about school and John's progress?

MOTHER: I haven't been very pleased. I think John can do much better. He's not talking well, although he does much better at home than at school according to what his teachers have told me. I think he can learn to talk very well.

TEACHER: It must be important for you to have John talk well.

MOTHER: Yet, it is. I don't want him talking with his hands or making those awful sounds that he does. They just really upset me.

TEACHER: I can understand that. It bothers me when I hear that "deafy" sound. I feel like a failure sometimes. Do you get that feeling, too?

MOTHER: Yes. I don't like to think about it or about what the future might bring.

TEACHER: There must have been a lot of tears for this child.

MOTHER: Yes, there were. I've had to do it all myself. I've done what everybody has asked me to do and he's still not talking well.

TEACHER: You sound very discouraged.

MOTHER: (Crying now) I am. I've put so much into this child, and he tries so hard, and I don't know what to do. (Long pause) What do you think about John?

TEACHER: I am concerned, too. I see him as a very tense child, also, who is trying very hard and starting to feel like a failure, much like his mother.

MOTHER: What do you think I should do?

TEACHER: You and I need to keep in touch and consider all the possibilities. Can you come in next Tuesday and watch John in class and see what I'm doing? Maybe you can suggest some things for me to do. I would also like to visit your home and see John in that setting. Would that be all right with you?

MOTHER: I'd like that very much.

TEACHER: Together we can begin to work out what is best to do. One thing we may want to consider is the possibility of changing John's school.

MOTHER: Does that mean that he'll have to talk with his hands?

TEACHER: That's a possibility we might consider. Right now, let's see what we can both do to make things better for John and you. I'll see you on Tuesday and we can talk some more then.

Summary

Federal legislation has placed increased pressure on parents and educators to participate jointly in the educational planning and monitoring process. That will require more sophisticated parents and a large increase in parent-education programs. Local parent groups will have to increase their responsibility toward maintaining informed parents. The various educational options—residential, day placement, and mainstreaming—all require different demands on educators and parents, and the schools will have to develop more parent programs. Educational decisions need to be seen as short-term arrangements, and must take into account personal and family needs. Parents and professionals need not be caught up in the methodology controversy, but both can seek the best approach for that particular child and family.

References

1. Meltzer, D. "Mainstreaming: As the Parent Sees It." *Soundings,* April, 1978.
2. Northern, J., and Downs, M. *Hearing in Children.* Baltimore, Maryland: Williams & Wilkins, 1974.
3. Ross, M. Model Educational Cascade for Hearing-Impaired Children. In Gary W. Nix (Ed.), *Mainstream Education of Hearing-Impaired Children and Youth.* New York: Grune & Stratton, 1976.
4. Ross, M. "Mainstreaming: Some Social Considerations." *Volta Review* 80:21-30, 1978.
5. Testut, E. W., and Baldwin, R. L. "Educational Options." *Volta Review* 79:281-286, 1977.

Epilogue

As I reread what I have written to avoid retrospective regrets of "I should have written . . . ," I realize how revolutionary a change I am advocating in the field of special education, with its concomitant need for parent counseling. I am asking for and seeking a shift of power—on both personal and political levels. It seems to me that the field of education of the handicapped is dominated by the cognitive and behavioral philosophies, with power clearly residing within the educational institution and the political bureaucracy. If the humanistic precepts suggested in this book are followed, power will revert back to the parents, to students in training programs, and to the handicapped individuals themselves; they will all be given more influence in determining what happens to them. I think that the passage of P.L. 94-142 is a very large step toward giving parents and the handicapped child real political power. It remains to be seen whether or not parents will learn to exercise their power.

If the humanistic revolution is followed through, the disenfranchised people in the system will be accorded their rights, the bureaucracy will become person-centered rather than institution-centered; teachers will teach *to* and *with* students, rather than *at* them; and bureaucrats will allow parents to have real power within the system. The revolution I have in mind will not be an armed revolt with much carnage (although a lot of confrontation must take place) but, rather, it will be what Rogers [1] refers to as the *quiet revolution*. The quiet revolution is:

— The physician who gives the parents ample time and really listens to them
— The administrator who actively solicits parental input and acts on it
— The teacher who tears up her lesson plan and lets the students guide their own learning
— The teacher who sees the child and parent beyond the issue of methodology
— The teacher who is concerned about the child's emotional health
— The educational plan that is written for the child rather than for the system
— The parent who refuses to be intimidated by the school and takes an active role in her child's education
— The professional training program that places increased importance on interpersonal skills
— The professional who places as much importance on his personal growth as he does in acquiring professional techniques
— People quietly standing up for what they believe in

One of my primary purposes in writing this book was to organize and clarify my last thirteen years of professional experience and personal growth. Writing this book has served that purpose very well. Another purpose in writing it was to incite you, the reader, to dare to be different, to begin asking "Why not?" to various kinds of questions, and to look at parents of handicapped children in a different way. Adlai Stevenson's eulogy for Eleanor Roosevelt— *She did not grumble about the darkness; she lit candles.* —has inspired me in my work and I hope that, in turn, this book has encouraged some readers to begin lighting candles.

Reference

1. Rogers, C. *On Personal Power.* New York: Delacorte, 1977.

Index

189